John Paul II
The Pope Who Understood

FÁTIMA

*The
Unprecedented Role of Fátima in the Course
of Recent World History and on
the Mission of John Paul II*

Eduardo Sigüenza

Queenship

PUBLISHING COMPANY
P.O. Box 220 • Goleta, CA 93116
(800) 647-9882 • (805) 692-0043 • Fax: (805) 967-5133
www.queenship.org

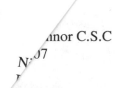

nor C.S.C

N⸱ 07

Library of Congress Number # 2007939947

Published by:
Queenship Publishing
P.O. Box 220
Goleta, CA 93116
(800) 647-9882 • (805) 692-0043 • Fax: (805) 967-5133
www.queenship.org

Printed in the United States of America

ISBN: 978-1-57918-326-3

Dedication

To God, whose infinite Mercy willed to send Our Lady to Fátima, to remind us of His Fatherly love and concern.

To the wonderful Mother of Our Lord, who obediently agreed to come down to the earth in 1917, in order to remind us of our part in the Heavenly Plan of Salvation.

To my wonderful guardian angel, who, obedient to his Creator, led me to the wonderful land of Fátima and to the spiritual sources that guided me, and that provided for the content of this work.

To all those anonymous brothers and sisters, whose prayers and sacrifices for me and for other sinners, have brought about the graces for my conversion and my spiritual journey.

To my earthly parents, who sacrificed themselves in order to send me to Marist primary and secondary schools, where my knowledge and appreciation for the Mother of God were first developed.

Finally, to all those friends who helped me by proofreading and editing my original works.

Table of Contents

Foreword

Fatima is perhaps the best known of all the Marian apparitions that have occurred. However, there are, as the present work demonstrates, historical roots that are little known, and which shed an interesting light on the apparitions.

Our Lady of Fatima told the visionaries that Jesus wanted to spread devotion to her Immaculate Heart, and that He wanted Russia in particular to be consecrated to her. But many centuries before the apparitions occurred, Portugal itself had, in effect undergone such a consecration.

At the time of King João IV, people did not yet speak of the Immaculate Heart of Mary. At that time, there was a debate going on among theologians as to whether the Immaculate Conception was part of the Catholic faith. (This dogma, which we now take for granted, would not be defined until 1854.) King João, the man responsible for recovering Portugal's independence from Spain, insisted that the University of Coimbra defend this doctrine. Furthermore, he required all the cities, villages and other locales in his kingdom take "Our Lady of the Conception" for their patroness. Finally, by a very solemn decree of 1646, he proclaimed Our Lady of the Conception patroness of his kingdoms and colonies.

As a sign of Mary's role, the king took the crown from his own head and placed it upon a statue of the Blessed Virgin. Thus, nearly 300 years before the apparitions at Fatima, Portugal itself had, in effect, been consecrated to the Immaculate Heart of Mary. What Mary requested at Fatima was, therefore, an extension to the rest of the world, and in particular to Russia, of what had already taken place in regard to Portugal!

As is demonstrated effectively in the present work, this is no doubt what prepared Portugal for the role entrusted to it at Fatima. We are all deeply indebted to Mr. Sigüenza for bringing this to our attention.

Edward D. O'Connor, C.S.C.
University of Notre Dame
South Bend, Indiana

Prologue

Does the world truly understand
the real secret Message of Fátima?

Unfortunately through the years, many Fátima devotees have placed so much emphasis on the unrevealed "third secret of Fátima" that they have failed to pay attention to the part of the message that had already been revealed to the world. During one of my summer-long visits to Fátima I had the opportunity to spend a whole summer in northern Portugal, in the very house where Sister Lucia had spent her summers while attending school. At this house (now owned by the Carmelite Order and reserved for retreats and discernment) I was able to dedicate a lot of time to the reading of the actual documents of Fátima, and it struck me that Fátima is the most misunderstood and underestimated Marian apparition by many. During the past 88 years, most people around the world have mistakenly assumed that the essence of the Fátima message could be summarized as a mere call to praying the Rosary and the wearing of the brown scapular, while overlooking the rest. They were wrong.

I first traveled to Fátima on October 13th 1991, only five months after John Paul II had made his second pilgrimage there on May 13th. Since then, I have been blessed with the opportunity of making nine additional pilgrimages to the blessed land of Our Lady, including the Beatification of the two little shepherds in the year 2000. One of the most inspiring experiences that I have ever witnessed during those pilgrimages to Fátima, was the response of the Portuguese people to Our Lady's pleas. While most of us foreign "pilgrims" usually arrive at the village in luxurious air-conditioned motorbuses and proceed to stay in hotels with our advanced no-risk reservations, the Portuguese pilgrims have a different concept of what a pilgrimage should be.

Looking out of my Fátima hotel room window on the eve of an anniversary of the apparitions, I witnessed the most touching scene. I beheld thousands of pilgrims traveling by foot, beginning to arrive by groups on their way to the Shrine. When I asked where all these walking people were coming from, I was stunned. I was informed that year after year, thousands of pilgrims from all over Portugal depart on foot from far away villages and towns with destination to Fátima. This is not due to a lack of motorized transportation, but to a spiritual choice that they make. Their arduous journey can even last over a week or two. Most of them are wearing sandals or humble footwear, not fancy hiking shoes. Some, though they could bring more, take no more bedding than an old newspaper. It is all part of the sacrifice! They come from all walks of life, entire families: grandparents and parents, teenagers and even children. I met a taxi driver from the northern Portuguese city of Braga, about two hundred kilometers from Fátima, who made the pilgrimage with his family every year. The Fátima Shrine authorities estimated in 2006 that more than 30,000 pilgrims were expected to make the long journey by foot for the anniversary celebrations in Fátima.[1]

Many walk a couple hundred kilometers or more, traveling under the hot sun during the day and in the chilling coolness of the evenings, taking only a few hours to rest by the side of the road. Through their previous experiences they have learned how to time their journey so as to arrive at the shrine on the vigil of the anniversary celebrations of the apparitions.

My amazement did not stop there! The most touching scene came when we went to the Shrine itself and observed the pilgrims' arrival in the plaza. While most of us foreign "pilgrims" upon our arrival at Fátima first run to secure accommodations and refresh ourselves from our journey, these Portuguese pilgrims, ignoring their sore legs and feet, steer straight to their Mother's shrine and begin to walk on their knees. Even more amazing is that most of them are smiling and praying the Rosary while doing it!

It was sad to witness how some foreign visitors frowned and even accused these humble people of "excessive devotion" and "extreme piety." I asked myself could these critics be right? Why do the pilgrims feel that they need to do all this walking? Why do they

1   Boletim Sala de Prensa, Santuario de Fátima May 11, 2006 www.santuario-fatima.pt

crawl painfully on their knees to the altar of Our Lady? Could this be wrong?

Then the answer came! These humble people have really understood the true message of Fátima: reparation! Most of them have read and are very familiar with the lives of the three little shepherds to whom Our Lady said, "but first you must offer many sacrifices," and they are trying to follow their example. The three children responded to our Lady's call by

The three little shepherds: Lucia, Francisco and Jacinta

making many sacrifices at their young tender age, for the conversion of sinners. They secretly chose to wear a rough piece of an old coarse rope tied around their little waists where no one could see it; they even slept with it on! This was their choice and no one knew about it, except Our Lady. During the fifth apparition she told them "God is very pleased with your sacrifices, but He does not desire you to wear the rope when you are sleeping. You should wear it only during the day." Obviously, God must also be pleased with the present sacrifices of His Portuguese children.

During the Beatification of the children, John Paul II reminded the pilgrims, "The Blessed Virgin came here to Fátima to ask men and women 'to stop offending God, Our Lord, who is already very offended'. It is a mother's sorrow that compels her to speak; the destiny of her children is at stake. For this reason she asks the little shepherds: 'Pray, pray much and make sacrifices for sinners; many souls go to hell because they have no one to pray and make sacrifices for them'."

But, to make sacrifices for sinners is something quite foreign to the modern Western mentality. These Portuguese children understood that the battle between their Heavenly Mother and the diabolical *ancient serpent* is at hand, and that Our Lady needs our prayers and also our sacrifices of reparation for the battle. While many curious outsiders have wasted time and money prying and trying to outguess a part of a secret which was not ours to know, the Portuguese have spent many years living the message of the part of the secret that Heaven wanted us to know: reparation through prayers and sacrifices!

The Message of Our Lady of Fátima to the world is probably one of the most significant messages from Heaven to humanity in the past 2000 years. To John Paul II, it was "the Marian Message" for the Third Millennium. Unfortunately, it seems to have been not fully grasped by a great majority of the modern Catholic faithful. Why? I don't believe that this has been a willful neglect on the part of anyone, but an inability that needs to be overcome. Unfortunately, most of us Catholics in the West have lacked the necessary background on world political events, on European History, on the monarchical system, and on Biblical Theology to fully appreciate the full, amazing dimension of the message at Fátima. In this short journey, we will try to discuss all these wonderful aspects.

1

John Paul II's Legacy and the Prophetic Secret of Fátima

Over a million pilgrims at the Fátima Shrine for the Beatification of Francisco and Jacinta

On May 13th of the year 2000, in an unexpected move, our former Bishop of Rome, Pope John Paul II traveled for his third and last visit to the holy shrine of Fátima in order to beatify two of the three child visionaries who had seen Our Lady there exactly 83 years ago. The third visionary, Sister Lucia, was also still alive then. This was an unprecedented move, because this was the long awaited *Jubilee Year 2000*, and all beatification and canonization ceremonies had been scheduled in Rome. Their beatification had originally been scheduled for Rome in April, yet, the enlightened Vicar of Christ, guided by the Holy Spirit considered that this specific beatification ceremony was important enough for it to be the exception of the *Jubilee Year*. Thus, it was re-scheduled for Fátima on the anniversary of the apparitions. Why?

Interestingly enough, even the canonization ceremony of the Polish nun, Sister Maria Faustina Kowalska, who was very dear to the Pope's heart, did not appear to merit another exception with a trip to the Holy Father's homeland. During that whole year every other canonization or beatification took place in Rome. Why was Portugal an exemption? Why did the Holy Father consider it so vital to bring the attention of the world to Fátima once again?

This was the Holy Father's third visit to the shrine of Fátima during his pontificate. His first visit had been on May 13, 1982, for the one-year anniversary of the attempt on his life. His second visit, on May 13, 1991 had commemorated ten years of that event. Now, over a million pilgrims, and Sister Lucia greeted him for the beatification ceremony. This was to be the last occasion that John Paul II and Sister Lucia would ever meet personally in this world. Their next meeting would have to take place in heaven in April of 2005.

The Essence of the Third part of the Secret of Fátima

Beatification pictures of Francisco and Jacinta

A year before the apparitions of Our Lady, Sister Lucia recalled that between April and October of 1916, an angel had appeared three times to the three visionaries, twice in the place known as the *Loca of the Cabeço* and another time, next to the well of Lucia's family home, inviting them to prayer and penance.

On May 13, 1917, three young children were tending a small flock in a rocky field called the *Cova da Iria*, in the outskirts of Fátima, of the municipality of *Ourém*, which today forms part of the diocese of *Leiria-Fátima*. They were called Lúcia of Jesus, who was 10 years of age, Francisco Marto aged 9, and Jacinta Marto, who was 7 years of age.

Around midday, after having prayed the Rosary, as they usually did, the children were entertaining themselves building a small house with loose stones, at the very same place where the Basilica is located today. Suddenly, they saw a bright light. Judging it to be lightning, they decided to leave for home immediately, but, soon below, another "lightning stroke" illuminated that space. They saw on top of a small Holm Oak tree (where today you find the little "Chapel of the Apparitions", a Lady brighter than the sun, from whose hands hung a white Rosary.

The Lady told the three little shepherds that it was necessary to pray very much and she invited them to come back to the *Cove of Iria* during five more consecutive months, on the 13th day, and at that very same hour. The young ones did as she requested, and on the 13th day of June, July, September and October, the Lady returned and spoke to them, in the *Cova da Iria*. On the 19th of August, the apparition took place in the small farm of *Valinhos*, some 500 meters from the place of *Aljustrel*, because, on the 13th day, the children had been deceived and taken by the Administrator of the Council, to *Vila Nova of Ourém*.

In the last apparition, of October 13th, with over 70,000 persons present, the Lady told them that she was the "Lady of the Rosary" and that they should build there a chapel in her honor. After the apparition, all of those present, including skeptic reporters, observed the miracle previously promised to the three children during the apparitions of July and September. The sun, resembling a silver disk, could be seen without difficulty. It rotated and spun about itself as a wheel of fire, and then seemed to precipitate itself towards the earth. Secular newspapers later reported, "The Sun danced in Fátima."

Later, after the two younger children had been taken to Heaven, and Lucia had become a Dorothean nun, Our Lady appeared to her again at the

Convent of *Pontevedra*, Spain. (On December 10, 1925 and on February 15, 1926) She then appeared on the night of June 13, 1929, at the Convent of Tuy, Spain, asking for the devotion of the First Five Saturdays - to pray the Rosary, to meditate on mysteries of the Rosary, to go to confession and to receive Holy Communion, in reparation for the sins committed against the Immaculate Heart of Mary. She also asked for the consecration of Russia to the Immaculate Heart. This request had already been made known by Our Lady on July 13, 1917, in the already revealed part of what has been called the "Secret of Fátima".

It was during the 1917 apparitions that Our Lady privately revealed to the children what has come to be known as "the Secret of Fátima." This secret is divided into three parts. The first two parts of the secret were soon revealed and published and were therefore known by the faithful. The third part of the secret was never revealed to the public by Sister Lucia. Later

it was written and sealed in an envelope by order of the then Bishop of Leiria-Fatima on January 3, 1944.

Before giving the sealed envelope containing the third part of the secret to the Bishop, Sister Lucia wrote on the outside of the envelope that it could be opened only after 1960, either by the Patriarch of Lisbon or the Bishop of Leiria. Archbishop Bertone asked: "Why only after 1960? Was it Our Lady who fixed that date?" Sister Lucia replied: "It was not Our Lady.

Sister Lucia, receiving communion from the Pope at the beatification.

I fixed the date because I had the intuition that before 1960 it would not be understood, but that only later would it be understood. Now it can be better understood. I wrote down what I saw; however it was not for me to interpret it, but for the Pope."[1] Sister Lucia must have known! She was the one entrusted by Heaven with the secret.

The Commissary of the Holy Office, Father Pierre Paul Philippe, with the agreement of Cardinal Alfredo Ottaviani, brought the envelope containing the third part of the secret of Fatima to Pope John XXIII on August 17th, 1959. "After some hesitation," His Holiness said, "We shall wait. I shall pray. I shall let you know what I decide."[2] It is reported that Pope John XXIII opened the sealed envelope and read the secret. He decided to place it back in the archives of the Vatican's *Congregation for the Doctrine of the Faith* where it remained hidden from the world until the year 2000.

Since 1917, millions of pilgrims have not ceased to visit the place of the *Cova da Iria* in Fátima. The pilgrims first came to visit on the 13th day of each month. Later on, they began to come on the vacation months of summer and winter. Today even more come on weekends and on weekdays, adding up to a total of four million pilgrims annually.

During the Beatification ceremony for Jacinta and Francisco of the year 2000, Pope John Paul II shocked the world. Through the mediation of Cardinal Angelo Sodano, in the presence of Sister Lucia, and before a crowd of a million and a quarter pilgrims, he revealed to the world the long awaited third part of the secret, which had been confided by the Lady of Heaven to the children 83 years before. Prior to the Beatification, the world had already learned the previous two parts of the secret. The first part spoke of the terrible vision of hell where the souls of poor sinners go. The second part of the secret revealed God's desire to establish in the world devotion to the Immaculate Heart of His Mother, to bring souls to salvation, and possible punishments if Our Lady's requests were not heeded. The third part had not been revealed to the world and had been entrusted in a sealed envelope only to the successor of Peter. Why? What was so grave about it?

---

1 "The Message of Fátima," Document. Archbishop Tarcicso Bertone, Congregation for the Doctrine of the Faith. July 2000.
2 "The Message of Fátima," Document. Archbishop Tarcicso Bertone, Congregation for the Doctrine of the Faith. July 2000.

The world's Reaction to the revelation of the Third Part of the Secret

Pope John Paul II among pilgrims at Saint Peter's Square

The first reaction of some to the release of the third part of the secret was to focus attention mainly on the assassination attempt on Pope John Paul II's life on May 13, 1981.

On this anniversary of Fátima, near 5:15 in the afternoon, the Pope was being driven in a jeep through a crowd of about 20,000 worshippers when four bullets fired at him from a 9mm pistol some 15 feet away. The Police immediately arrested a 23-year-old man who said he was a Turkish citizen named Mehmet Ali Agca, an escaped terrorist who had vowed to kill the Pope. The Pope was rushed to the Gemelli Hospital in Rome, where he was operated on for 6 hours and hospitalized for 22 days. On May 17, John Paul II recited the Angelus from his bed at *Gemelli Hospital*, which was heard by all the concerned faithful all over Saint Peter's Square:

Pope John Paul II being shot in Rome on May 13, 1981

"Pray for the brother who shot me, whom I have sincerely forgiven."

After the assassination attempt of May 13, 1981, the Pope himself said that it was "a Mother's hand that guided the bullet's path", enabling the Pope to escape death. Agca shot to kill. One of the bullets passed through the Holy Father's body, wounding him in the stomach but it seemed to have been miraculously redirected so as to miss most of his vital organs. The bullet then fell between the Pope and monsignor Dziwisz. On the occasion of a visit to Rome by the then Bishop of Leiria-Fatima, the Pope gave him the bullet which had remained in the jeep after the assassination attempt, so that it might be kept in the shrine. By the Bishop's decision, the bullet was later set in the crown of the statue of Our Lady of Fatima.

In his last book before his death, the Holy Father said: "Could I forget that the event in Saint Peter's Square took place on the day and at the hour when the first appearance of the Mother of Christ to the poor little peasants has been remembered for over sixty years at Fátima in Portugal? For, in everything that happened to me on that very day, I felt that extraordinary motherly protection and care, which turned out to be stronger than the deadly bullet."[3]

Around Christmas 1983, John Paul II made public his pardon by visiting his attacker Ali Agca in prison. Their meeting was private and the pope and his would-be-assassin spoke at length. The pope only shared that "Ali Agca, as everyone knows, was a professional assassin. This means that the attack was not his own initiative, it was someone else's idea; someone else had commissioned him to carry it out."[4] If Agca exposed the name of his "employer" to the pope, he never revealed it.

The Pope visits Mehmet Ali Agca in prison in 1983

The Holy Father did disclose that, "In the course of our conversation it became clear that Ali Agca was still wondering how the attempted assassination could possibly have failed. He had planned it meticulously

3 John Paul II, *Memory And Identity.* Rizzoli International Publications, New York. Page 163.
4 Ibid.

… his perplexity had led him to the religious question. He wanted to know about the secret of Fátima, and what the secret was… Ali Agca had probably sensed that over and above his own power, over and above the power of shooting and killing, there was a higher power. He then began to look for it. I hope and pray that he found it." [5] Twelve years later, from his Turkish prison cell, Agca would beg the authorities to be allowed to attend and to pay his respects at Pope John Paul II's funeral on April 8, 2005. (He was finally released from prison on January 12th, 2006.)

The Vatican document, *The Message of Fátima,* concerning the secret informs us that while both Pope John XXIII and Pope Paul VI also read the secret on March 27, 1965, Pope John Paul II did not read it until *after* the assassination attempt on May 13, 1981. Recuperating in the Gemelli Hospital in Rome, he asked for the envelope containing the third part of the secret.[6] This third part had been revealed to Sister Lucia in a mystical way:

> *After the two parts which I have already explained, at the left of Our Lady and a little above, we saw an Angel with a flaming sword in his left hand; flashing, it gave out flames that looked as though they would set the world on fire; but they died out in contact with the splendor that Our Lady radiated towards him from her right hand: pointing to the earth with his right hand, the Angel cried out in a loud voice: 'Penance, Penance, Penance!'. And we saw in an immense light that is God: 'something similar to how people appear in a mirror when they pass in front of it' a Bishop dressed in White 'we had the impression that it was the Holy Father'. Other Bishops, Priests, men and women Religious going up a steep mountain, at the top of which there was a big Cross of rough-hewn trunks as of a cork-tree with the bark; before reaching there the Holy Father passed through a big city half in ruins and half trembling with halting step, afflicted with pain and sorrow, he prayed for the souls of the corpses he met on his way; having reached the top of the mountain, on his knees at the foot of the big Cross he was killed by a group of soldiers who fired bullets and arrows at him, and in the same way there died one after another the other Bishops, Priests, men and women Religious, and various lay people of different ranks and positions.*

---

5 John Paul II, *Memory And Identity.* Rizzoli International Publications, New York. Page 163.
6 Ibid.

> *Beneath the two arms of the Cross there were two Angels each with a crystal aspersorium in his hand, in which they gathered up the blood of the Martyrs and with it sprinkled the souls that were making their way to God.*

Before the Vatican unveiled the third part of the Secret, papal envoys visited Sister Lucia in her cloistered Portuguese convent to seek her opinion of the Vatican's interpretation and her permission to reveal it. When asked: Is the principal figure in the vision the pope? Sister Lucia replied that it was.

"According to the interpretation of the 'little shepherds', which was also confirmed recently by Sister Lucia, 'the Bishop clothed in white' who prays for all the faithful is the Pope. As he makes his way with great difficulty towards the Cross amid the corpses of those who were martyred (Bishops, priests, men and women Religious and many lay people), he too falls to the ground, apparently dead, under a hail of gunfire."[7]

The Pope was certainly the main figure in the third part, but also there is contained in this message the persecution of the faithful, including other witnesses and martyrs to the faith in the 20th Century. These came about because of the failure of the world to return to Jesus Christ of the Gospels.

Many people who had expected the message to contain apocalyptic cataclysms and sensationalistic reports of global destruction were somewhat disappointed. Some hardened skeptics still maintained that the secret continued to remain unrevealed. Fortunately, Sister Lucia herself had been invited to leave her convent and come to Fátima for the beatification of her two cousins. She was sitting right behind the Pope when the secret was announced, and she confirmed it!

On September 21st, 2007, at the official presentation of Cardinal Bertone's book, *"The Last Fátima Visionary,"* Archbishop Loris Capovilla, Pope John XXIII's private secretary, said that there is no fourth secret. He is the only living witness who was present when John XXIII opened and read the third secret in 1959 at Castel Gandolfo. The 91-year-old prelate said: *"It never even entered my mind that there could be a fourth secret. No one ever said such a thing to me nor did I ever claim any such thing."* [8]

---

7 "The Message of Fátima," Document. Archbishop Tarcisco Bertone, Congregation for the Doctrine of the Faith.
8 *"No More Fatima Secrets, Says Cardinal"* Zenit News Agency. September 24, 2007

Sister Lucia's Mission on earth
Shall I stay here alone?

During the second apparition, young Lucia asked the Lady from Heaven if they were going to heaven. Our Lady responded: "Yes, I will take Jacinta and Francisco soon but you must stay a while longer. Jesus wants to use you to make me known and loved. He wants to establish in the world the devotion to my Immaculate Heart." The child respectfully cried, "Shall I stay here alone?" and the compassionate Queen of Heaven responded "No daughter. Are you suffering a great deal? Do not be downhearted.

I shall never leave you. My Immaculate Heart will be your refuge and the way that will lead you to God." Both Jacinta and Francisco died within two and a half years after the apparitions. Francisco died on April 4th 1919 and Jacinta on February 20th 1920. Little Lucia, without her beloved cousins remained in the world and continued her mission of love for an additional eighty seven years.

But Lucia's life was never going to be the same. In the likeness of Saint Bernadette of Lourdes, her privileged eyes had

Little Lucia Dos Santos 1917

beheld a vision of a beautiful visitor from the Divine World, and there was a price to pay. Our Lady had specially asked the young shepherdess to learn to read. Should this have served as a foretelling that her future life was not going to continue in the grazing fields of Fátima? Her life began to change almost immediately. After the painful departure of her little cousins for Heaven, other changes began to become evident. The thousands of pilgrims, thirsty for a taste of Heaven, began to flock unceasingly into the little village and into the life of the little visionary. Her child life was anything but normal. A constant flow of people would arrive, asking to see, hear or touch "the little girl who saw the Virgin." Some would ask for her intercession for miracles, others wanted to be blessed by her. Many wanted to hear the whole story again from the lips of the visionary and form their own opinion. Yet, some skeptics were seeking to find a reason to doubt through the formulation of tricky questions. All this was very overwhelming for a humble ten-year-old peasant girl who had yet to learn to read and write.

The Portuguese Catholic Church was aware of all this and was striving to offer a solution, a solution that once again would modify the life of young Lucia forever. When Lucia was about fifteen years of age, the local Bishop José Alves Correia da Silva had the young shepherdess brought to his office in Leiria. After a long conversation with the visionary, he suggested for her to leave Fátima and to go to the northern Portuguese city of Oporto, to study and to be educated in a boarding school. But this was not the hardest part. The bishop suggested that Lucia had to study somewhere where she was not known. For this to be possible, at the school in Oporto the young visionary would have to remain in complete anonymity and obscurity. She was not to speak about the apparitions to anyone, nor about her parents or family. Her visitation would be limited to the ladies appointed by the

**Humble house of Lucia's family
in the hamlet of Aljustrel, Fátima.**

bishop to care for her. Her mail would be only to her mother and should be directed through the Vicar of Olival who would then be responsible for delivering them to her mother. But there was still another more painful requirement. She would not return to Fátima for the holidays nor for any other purpose without the bishop's permission.[9]

According to Sister Lucia, words could never express properly the

9 *"The Intimate Life of Sister Lucia,"* Father Antonio Maria Martins & Fr. Robert Fox Fátima Family Apostolate, 2001. Page 107.

agonizing sorrow that this proposition brought to her teenage heart. She would lose touch with her beloved sisters and other relatives to whom she would not be able to write. She would have to abandon the hometown village where she had spent her happy childhood. She would never again walk through the fields where she and her little cousins played and where they met Our Lady. At first, the pain in her heart led her to believe that the only response was to refuse. After all, this humble little peasant girl did not even know where this city of Oporto was. Her letters home during the early years show that the young visionary's body went to Porto, but her soul remained in Fátima.[10]

The young shepherdess also knew that the mission she had been entrusted with was at stake. The Church was just beginning to investigate the veracity of the apparitions. Although the 70,000 witnesses gave a tremendous testimony, no official decision had yet been made. The constant scrutiny of the thousands of curious visitors could definitely hinder the Church's investigation, and the Lady's mission. Lucia knew that at every interview she ran the risk of having her words twisted or misinterpreted. She knew that accepting the bishop's proposition would involve tremendous suffering, but then again she could not forget the words of the Lady during the first apparition: "You will have a lot to suffer then, but God's grace will be your comfort." In the early morning of June 16, 1921 young Lucia left her native village for the northern city of Oporto and her life would never be same again. Her early letters home reveal the heartbreaking homesickness in her heart, yet her obedience to the bishop prevailed. Pope John Paul II wrote: "For Lucia, the visit by the Virgin to her and her cousins Francisco and Jacinta, in Fátima in 1917, was the beginning of a mission to which she remained faithful to the end of her days. Sister Lucia leaves us an example of great faithfulness to the Lord, and of joyous obedience to His divine will."[11]

In 1928 Sister Lucia took first vows as a religious of Saint Dorothy and made her perpetual vows in 1934, assuming the name Sister Maria Lucia of Jesus and the Immaculate Heart. In 1948, desiring a more contemplative life, she transferred to the cloistered convent of the Carmelites in Coimbra, Portugal.

Eighty-four years after the sad day that she departed from Fátima,

---

10 *"The Intimate Life of Sister Lucia,"* Father Antonio Maria Martins & Fr. Robert Fox Fátima Family Apostolate, 2001. Page 107
11 John Paul II: Papal Message at Sister Lucia's Funeral, delivered by Cardinal Bertone on February 16, 2005.

after having lived a dedicated cloistered life for the last 48 years, she was again visited by the Lady from Heaven. On Sunday February 13th, 2005 Sister Lucia of the Immaculate Heart left this world at the age of 97, to join her two cousins Jacinta and Francisco in their eternal home

The Vatican reported that on the eve of her death, the Holy Father had sent a fax to Sister Lucia expressing his closeness and the assurance of his prayers so that she might "experience this moment of pain, suffering and sacrifice with the spirit of Easter", and he ended his message imparting his blessing to her. The Carmelite sisters who were at Sister Lucia's side during the final moments of her life said the Sister Lucia read the Holy Father's message.[12]

Sister Lucia died in her convent cell surrounded by her sisters in religion, by the bishop of Coimbra and by the doctors and nurse attending her. The Portuguese Government declared February 15th, the date of her funeral, as a national day of mourning. Even political candidates suspended

Sr. Lucia's body behind the cloister grid at her Carmelite convent in Coimbra.

their electoral campaigns. The Holy Father sent Cardinal Tarcisio Bertone to Portugal to officiate at the funeral Mass.

Tens of thousands of people with flowers arrived from all over Portugal and other countries to bid farewell to Sister Lucia and participate in the funeral. An uninterrupted pilgrimage of people surrounded her exposed casket with tears, affection and prayer. Later, thousands more waved white handkerchiefs as her coffin passed from the church to the final burial place at the Carmelite convent. The last of the three little shepherds of Fátima was finally home. Cardinal Bertone revealed that he had last visited Sister

---

12 http://www.ewtn.com/vnews/getstory.asp?number=53908

Lucia in November 2003, and had told her that he would come to visit her again. "She told me that I would not see her alive again, but that I would only come to bless her casket. She knew even this." He added: "I am not saying this was a prophecy, but it was simply the truth."[13]

The Pope's message read: "I like to think that Sister Lucia, in her transit from earth to heaven, was welcomed by the One whom she saw at Fátima so many years ago. May the Most Holy Virgin now accompany the soul of her devoted daughter to the beatific encounter with the divine Bridegroom."[14]

We have no reason to doubt that this same Heavenly Queen also returned 48 days later to the Vatican, to welcome the soul of her most devoted son! On April 2 of the year of the Lord 2005, at 9:37 p.m., as the first Saturday of the month was coming to an end, the beloved pastor of the Church, John Paul II, passed from this world to the Father. He could finally, in the company of the three little shepherds, contemplate personally the heavenly eyes of the Lady who appeared in Fátima, whom he served faithfully and whom he always called "mother."

At Sister Lucia's request, her body remained buried at the Carmelite convent for one year. On February 19th, 2006, her precious remains were transferred to her final resting place next to the tombs of her two little cousins Francisco and Jacinta inside the Basilica at the Shrine of Fátima. The transfer ceremony from Coimbra to Fátima was televised in Portugal and through Catholic channels in the United States. The Fatima faithful were ecstatic. Sister Lucia had finally returned to Fátima.

Portugal and the Events at Fátima

Today, Portugal is a small European nation of about 50,000 square miles, with a population of nearly 10,000,000 people. It lies west of Spain within the Iberian Peninsula, facing the Atlantic Ocean. Its independence as a nation dates from the year 1138 AD. It is a land of seafaring people and explorers. Due to its geographic location, its livelihood and industry have largely depended on the sea. The Catholic faith survived the invasion of the Muslims and the Moors from about 711 until 1249. The Protestant Reformation had very little effect in the country, which today is over 93% Catholic.

13 "The Vatican Letter", *Today's Catholic* March 6, 2005 page 17.
14 John Paul II: Papal Message at Sister Lucia's Funeral, delivered by Cardinal Bertone on February 16, 2005.

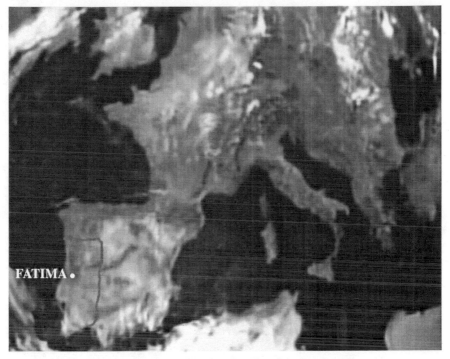

Portugal's location in the Iberian Peninsula.

King Afonso Henriques (1143-1185) the first king of independent Portugal, declared himself a "soldier of Saint Peter" and a "captain of the Church" under the command of the Pope, to whom he took an oath of fidelity. All those in military orders accompanying him to battle had taken vows to fight for Christ.[15]

Throughout its history, Portugal has proven to be not only a country strong in its Catholic faith, but also in its devotion to the Mother of God. Such Catholic faith has not been without tremendous trials and suffering. Some past anti-religious governments, led by secret societies, and internal enemies of the Church (such as the Marquis of Pombal in the 1700s), have formulated unjust and arbitrary laws which aimed to destroy the unity of faith between Portugal and the Catholic Church. The suffering of the Portuguese people has been tremendous. The Catholic Church has also suffered greatly. Nevertheless, the faith has always survived and the majority of the Portuguese faithful have continued to be an example of

---

15 *Fátima in the Light of History*, by Costa Brochado. Bruce Publishing Co. MI 1955. Page 2.

Catholic devotion in the world. Today, the Portuguese government enjoys friendly diplomatic relationships with the Holy See, and the recent national mourning during Sister Lucia's death was a clear testimony of this.

Although you can still find some who might make a claim to skepticism or non-belief, the fact remains that for the majority of Portugal, the events of Fátima and the miracle seen by 70,000 have come to be an undeniable part of their nation's history. Despite some past government opposition, most Portuguese school children are familiar with the events that took place at Fátima in 1917. Fortunately, such events also included a "maternal" catechesis from Heaven.

2

Fátima... A Catechesis from Heaven

The message of Fátima seems to be another love letter from Heaven written in code to be understood gradually by those simple enough to read it on their knees. Its first dimension reveals that in Fátima, *the Lady of Heaven came as a catechist*. She revealed in a simple form for the Portuguese people all those teachings of faith that would be put into doubt by many modern theologians in the Twentieth Century.

Monument of the apparition of the angel to the children

The Teachings of the Angel

Some of the faithful are also unaware that before the apparitions of Our Lady to the children in 1917, God sent a precursor, an angel to prepare the children for the coming of the Queen of Heaven. The angel came three times during 1916, once in the spring, then in the summer and finally in the fall. During these three appearances, the angel prepared the children spiritually for the catechesis that was to come. In the spring, he revealed to them the amazing redemptive power found in *the adoration of God*. In the summer, he instructed them on the *value of suffering*, and in the autumn, the teachings climaxed when he instructed them on the awesome value of *Eucharistic Reparation*. In the following statements taken from the documents written by Sister Lucia, we find many teachings filled with simple heavenly truths.

1. **The Existence and intercession of Guardian Angels**: In the first angelic apparition in 1916, the angel said to the children: "You will thus draw down peace on your country. I am its <u>Angel Guardian, the Angel of Portugal</u>. Above all, accept with submission the suffering which the Lord will send you."[16]

2. **The True Presence of Christ in the Eucharist:** About the third angelic apparition to the three children, Sister Lucia revealed that: "We sprang up and beheld the angel. He was holding a chalice in his left hand, with the Host suspended above it, from which some drops of blood fell into the chalice... Then the Angel added, 'Take and drink the Body and Blood of Jesus Christ, horribly outraged by ungrateful men. Make reparation for their crimes and console Our Lord.... Jesus Christ <u>present</u> in all the tabernacles of the world.'"

3. **The Truth of the Dogma of the Trinity:** Also, sister Lucia writes that during the third angelic apparition: "The angel <u>knelt down</u> beside us and made us repeat three times: 'Most Holy Trinity, Father, Son and Holy Spirit, I adore you profoundly, and I offer You the most precious Body, Blood, Soul and Divinity <u>of Jesus Christ present in all the tabernacles of the world</u>'..."

4. **The Proper Reverence by Creatures before the Blessed Sacrament:** During this same apparition: "Leaving the chalice suspended in the air, the angel <u>knelt</u> down beside us...Once again, he <u>prostrated</u> himself on the ground and repeated with us, three times more the same prayer...and then disappeared." (Today many Catholics struggle at even the simple gesture of genuflecting. If an angel, a heavenly creature, prostrates himself before the Blessed Sacrament, why should not we?)

5. **The Power of the Rosary for the Salvation of the World:** During the May 13th apparition, Our Lady requested: "'Pray the <u>Rosary</u> every day in order to obtain peace for the world and the end of the war.'" During the July apparition she added: "<u>Continue to pray the Rosary</u> every day in honor of Our Lady of the Rosary, in order to obtain peace

---

16 *In Sister Lucia's Own Words*. (Memoirs of Sister Lucia) Volume 1. Secretariado Dos Pastorinhos, Fátima, Portugal.

for the world and the end of the war, because <u>only she can help you</u>."

6. **The Call for Devotion to the Immaculate Heart of Mary:** During her second apparition Our Lady said: "Jesus wants to make use of you to make me known and loved. He wants to establish in the world devotion to my <u>Immaculate Heart</u>." "I will never forsake you. My Immaculate Heart will be your refuge and the way that will lead you to God."

7. **The Existence of Heaven and Purgatory:** Sister Lucia tells us that during the first apparition of Our Lady: "I remembered to ask about the two girls who had died recently: 'Is Maria das Neves in heaven?' - 'Yes, she is.' (She was about sixteen years old) - 'And Amelia?' – Our Lady responded: 'She will be in <u>Purgatory</u> until the end of the world'."

8. **The Existence of Hell:** During the third apparition, Our Lady spoke after showing the children the vision of hell: "You have seen <u>hell</u> where the souls of poor sinners go. To save them, God wants to establish in the world devotion to my Immaculate Heart." Fourth apparition: "Pray, pray very much, and make sacrifices for sinners; for <u>many souls go to hell</u>, because there are none to sacrifice and pray for them."

9. **The Seriousness of sin:** Sister Lucia reports that during the last apparition: "Looking very sad, Our Lady said: 'Do not offend the Lord our God any more, because He is already so much <u>offended</u>.'" And on the Third apparition: "The war is going to end; but if people don't cease <u>offending</u> God, a worse one will break out during the pontificate of Pius IX." This was a reference to World War II, and was conditional on the people's response.

10. **The Consecration of Russia to the Immaculate Heart:** During the July apparition: "To prevent this, (wars, famine and persecutions) I shall come to ask for the consecration of Russia to my Immaculate Heart and the communion of reparation on the first Saturdays. If my requests are heeded, Russia will be converted and there will be peace; if not she will spread her errors throughout the world causing wars and persecutions of the Church...."

11. **The Authority of the Pope**: Also during the July apparition Our Lady promised: "In the end, my Immaculate Heart will triumph. The <u>Holy Father</u> will consecrate Russia to me, and she will be converted, and a period of peace will be granted to the world." Obviously, the Holy Father's role was very important in Heaven's plan.

12. **The Importance of Men's prayer in Heaven's plan.** During Our Lady's first apparition, Francisco sadly complained that he was not able to see nor hear the Lady. Our Lady responded to the other two children, "tell him to say the Rosary and then he will see me". Francisco did as he was told and soon his eyes were contemplating the Heavenly beauty of Our Lady. What was the reason for this? Was Francisco less worthy in the eyes of Our Lady? This is very doubtful. It has been suggested that the reason for this condition was, that in those days good Portuguese men would easily fall in the trap of believing that praying the Rosary was the task reserved for the pious women and not for them. This was not meant as a cruel test for Francisco, but as a reminder for Francisco and for all men that the Hearts of Jesus and Mary were attentive to their prayers as well.

How about this for a lesson in Catechism from Heaven? It is a lot more than just a reminder about the Rosary and the Scapular, isn't it? For the Portuguese faithful, the events of Fátima are part of their nation's history. If like many Portuguese, one reads and is familiar with the documents of Fátima, there can be no doubt regarding what Heaven says about the Eucharist, about the primacy of the Pope and about sin. By now, we begin to realize that there is more to the Message of Fátima than just praying the Rosary. Actually, there still is *even more!*

October Thirteenth and Saint Joseph

One very little known fact is the role of St. Joseph during the apparition of October 13, 1917. On September 13, 1917, Our Lady announced to the children "In October Saint Joseph will come with the child Jesus to bless the world." While the 70,000 pilgrims were watching the miracle of the sun, the children were witnessing another supernatural reality. Sister Lucia related:

**Saint Joseph and the Child Jesus
at the Shrine of Sameiro**

"Here... is the reason that I cried out to the people to look at the sun. My aim was not to call their attention to the sun, because I was not even aware of their presence... When Our Lady disappeared in the immense distance of the firmament, beside the sun we saw Saint Joseph with the Child Jesus and Our Lady robed in white with a blue mantle. St. Joseph and the Child Jesus seemed to bless the world, for they made the sign of the cross with their hands."

Many remember October 13, 1917 as the day on which the sun danced. Very few realize that it was also the anniversary of the day that Saint Joseph came with the Child Jesus and blessed the world. This magnificent event had been announced a month in advance. One can wonder which one was the greatest gift: the miracle, which the people saw, or the reality, which the children witnessed!

Our Lady's Seventh coming to Fátima

Another often-overlooked historical fact of Fátima is the announcement of Our Lady's seventh coming: ***Despois voltarei ainda aqui uma setima vez.*** ("Afterwards I shall still return here a seventh time.") During 1917, Our Lady publicly appeared to the children six times, from May 13th to

October 13th. During her first Our Lady said to Lucia: "I want you to come here for six consecutive months, on the thirteenth day at the same time. Afterwards I shall still return here a seventh time."[17] Curiously, this phrase was not included in the earlier reports about the events because it was only revealed by Sister Lucia in obedience to the bishop, in her fourth written memoir.

Excerpt from Sister Lucia's own writing in Portuguese.

A key term in Our Lady's announcement is the word "here". Many have interpreted Our Lady's seventh visit as being the one that took place on **December 10th of 1925**, when Our Lady appeared to sister Lucia and asked for the sacramental reparation of Confession and Holy Communion on First Saturdays. That visit, however, took place in the convent of Pontevedra, Spain, not in Fátima. Others hold that it was Our Lady's apparition of **June 13, 1929,** to Sister Lucia in which she asked the Pope and bishops of the world for the consecration of Russia to her Immaculate Heart. Again, this took place in the Dorothean Convent of Tuy, a Spanish town on the border with Portugal. Neither of these apparitions seems to fulfill Our Lady's statement, "I shall still return here," which implies a return to the Cove in Fátima.

A footnote added to *Sister Lucia's Memoirs* suggests that this predicted *Seventh time* might have taken place on the morning of June 16, 1921, when Sister Lucia went back to the Cove to bid farewell to Fátima on her way to the convent. This would have been one more of the many personal visits of Our Lady to Sister Lucia. However, this theory seems contradicted by Sister's Lucia's words in her manuscripts from her Spanish convent. "After six years of real trial (since 1917) it was on this day, August 26, 1923, that the Virgin Mary first visited me again."[18] According to this, Our Lady did not appear to her at the Cove in 1921. As to whether the *seventh apparition* at the Cove foretold by Our Lady took place during Sister

---

17 Fourth Memoir *In Sister Lucia's Own Words.*
18 *The Intimate Life of Sister Lucia.* Fr. Antonio Maria Martins & Fr. Robert Fox Fátima Family Apostolate 2001. Page 118.

Lucia's lifetime or not, she never announced it. One can only wonder, why did Our Lady prophesy this *seventh apparition* so solemnly?

With the recent death of Sister Lucia, many disappointed hearts wonder, "Did Our Lady forget her promise?" But a careful reading of Our Lady's words may reveal another insight. Although the faithful have always assumed that Our Lady meant a seventh apparition to Sister Lucia, Our Lady's actual words, "I shall return <u>here</u>", never specified that such a visit would be a personal apparition to Sister Lucia. This prophesied *Seventh visit* continues to remain in the amazing mystery of Fátima.

But in Portugal the Dogma of Faith will always be preserved

During a careful reading of the Fátima documents and the *Memoirs of Sister Lucia,* one also discovers a phrase spoken by Our Lady, which has not received the attention it deserves. Right after revealing the three parts of the secret to the children, Our Lady concluded her message with *but in Portugal the dogma of faith will always be preserved.*

I remember being

John Paul II arriving in Fátima for the third time on May 13, 2000

puzzled with this foretelling statement by the Mother of God. Since Our Lady from Heaven does not come to earth to deliver unimportant information, we must realize that this is in itself a Marian Prophecy. First, what does it actually mean? Does it imply that the humble Portuguese people would always pray and have faith? This simplistic interpretation misses a key word: *Dogma*, the infallible teaching of the Church, which is connected to the presence of the Holy Father, God's appointed with the "keys of the Kingdom", to be the infallible Interpreter of the faith.

The late James Cardinal Gibbons once pointed out that the "The Council clearly declares that Immaculate doctrine has always been <u>preserved</u> and preached in the Roman See."[19] By this, he was stressing the need of a God-given interpreter for the proper understanding of the faith. He explained, "what good is the Constitution, without a Chief Justice to interpret it and apply it properly? The Constitution itself would become a dead letter." [20]

Cardinal Gibbons concluded, "Of what use to you is the objective infallibility of the Bible without an infallible interpreter?"[21] Who would protect us from confusion and division? The present existence in the world of over 25,000 different Christian sects is a sobering testimony to this! What is Our Lady telling Portugal? Even more important, what is Our Lady telling the world about Portugal? Why did she use the word *Dogma*? The answer to this still resides in the amazing mystery of Fátima.

The most intriguing part of those words is contained in its other dimension! If these words contain a special Heavenly promise for Portugal, we should ask ourselves, why? Why Portugal? What has Portugal done right that other nations could imitate? What else can we learn from the Portuguese believers? We will continue to discuss this ahead, but before we continue, let us make a short biblical study that illuminates the importance and the apocalyptic call of Fátima.

The Meaning of the Thirteenth Day of the Month and Fátima

Since Sister Lucia's recent death on February 13, 2005, a widespread discussion began regarding the hidden meaning of the number 13. This was due to the fact the Blessed Virgin Mary promised to appear to Lucia and her two little cousins on the 13th of each month, and that Pope John Paul II's life was spared on May 13th, 1981. After Sister Lucia's death, Cardinal Bertone was asked to comment: "The fact that the number 13 connects all the apparitions and was the date of the attempted assassination of the pope is something more than a simple coincidence, I think," the Cardinal said. "In the same way, I think it is a heavenly sign that the Madonna called Sister

---

19 Gibbons, James Cardinal, *The Faith of Our Fathers*, NY: John Murphy Company, 83rd Edition. May 1, 1917, p.128 (underline added).
20 Ibid., pp 124.
21 Ibid., pp. 134.

The 264th Keeper of the Dogma of Faith in Rome.

Lucia to herself precisely on the 13th of February." He added that people should remember the 13th of each month "not out of superstition," but simply because God and the Blessed Virgin Mary had done extraordinary things on that date in the past. [22]

This obviously demonstrates that, contrary to the widespread ridiculous superstition of modern times against the number "13", God sometimes does reveal his involvement and his will to us through the symbolism of numbers. We should not forget that next to the twelve apostles, Our Lady was the "thirteenth member" present at the birth of the Church on Pentecost Day.

---

22 "The Vatican Letter", *Today's Catholic* March 6, 2005 page 17.

3

FROM GENESIS TO FÁTIMA

When God decided to create the world, He prepared it with all the love that a father has in preparing a nursery room for His firstborn child. He placed stars on the ceiling, decorated it with lights and even included the little "horsies" and the rest of the animals. After giving life to His first son and before the formation of His first daughter, He entrusted the man with the dominion and government of all the Creation.

The Creator used several clear symbolic actions to communicate to His first human son that he, and not God, was to have responsibility for the beautiful nursery room. Instead of naming the animals Himself, God brought them to the man so that he, as their ruler, would name them. The Lord told Adam "fill the earth and subdue it; and <u>have dominion</u> over the fish of the sea and over the birds of the air and <u>over every living thing that moves upon the earth</u>." It was God's will for man to be the one who named everything.[23]

He commanded him to "rule" over all of the earth. Thus man was given jurisdiction and authority over God's Creation as the ruler of the world.

Later in Scripture, Saint Paul clearly holds Adam principally responsible for the fall of *both* of our first parents. He said, "For as in Adam all die, so also in Christ shall all be made alive."[24] Why? It is because of the jurisdiction that had been given to him by God during his original solitude. Scrip-

23 Genesis 2: 19- 20.
24 1 Corinthians 15: 22.

ture reports that before the creation of Eve, "The Lord God took the man and put him in the Garden of Eden to till it and guard it [25]. Obviously, the command "to guard" would have been senseless and useless if there had not been something or "someone" from whom to guard the Garden! Adam had been entrusted to guard everything and everyone in the Garden, *including* his beloved spouse. With jurisdiction comes authority, but also responsibility.

Man was given the trust and the responsibility to have dominion over an earth blessed by God. Unfortunately, a slave cannot be a ruler, and God's first human child, through his sin of pride and disobedience, became a slave of the ruler of darkness, thus surrendering this rule to the enemy of God.

The Biblical Jurisdiction given to Man and the Call for Consecration at Fátima

We have seen how our faithful and fatherly God respects the jurisdiction over the earth that He once gave to man. Jesus Himself confirmed this. During the temptations in the desert, the Devil took Our Lord to a very high mountain, and showed him all the kingdoms of the world and the glory that was theirs; and he said to him, "To you I will give all this authority and their glory; for it has been delivered to me, and I give it to whom I will. If you, then, will worship me, it shall all be yours."[26] Although Jesus could read through the deceit of Satan's lies, this time Our Lord never challenged his claim to all the kingdoms of the world. Why? Who surrendered to him this authority over them? Adam did, when he became a slave of sin!

As the Risen Lord was ascending to heaven He knew that He was leaving his disciples in a world which was still under the evil power of the adversary. This is why He prayed for them to His Father: "I do not pray that You should take them out of the world, but that You should keep them from the evil one."[27] Our Lord even referred to the Devil by the title *"the ruler of this world."[1]*

Disobedience brings about disobedience. God's creation was no longer under the authority of a God-fearing man but of a diabolical master. Death

---

1 John 12:31. "Now is the time of judgement on this world; now
the ruler of the world will be driven out" (Douay Rheims version)
25 Book of Genesis 2:15 "And The Lord God took the man and put him in the garden of Eden to till it and keep it."
26 Luke 4: 6-7.
27 John 17: 15.

had entered the world. At this point, creation seemed to rebel against man, and even the animals no longer respected him or obeyed him. Some even became a dangerous threat to man. What was God's response to this?

Despite Jesus' victory at the Resurrection, the fallen angel retains his evil power, which he exercises against the disciples and the Church.[28] *After restoring us to the Father's friendship and breaking the power of death,* Our Lord ascends to the Father leaving His Church in the midst of spiritual warfare. The "prince of this world" is still at large, but the Son of God knows that this "creaturely" battle is not His to undertake. His mission of salvation is over, and His triumph over Death has been accomplished.[29] The personal battle against the evil creature must be fought by the "Woman and her seed." This battle is the mission assigned to His Mother!

The Battle between the Serpent and the Woman

Why is the role of Mary so important in the final redemption of the fallen children of Eve? She is only a humble creature! We must not forget that the original wound against God's beloved creation came through the evil prompting of a proud and hateful "creature," Satan. The Devil, in his inability to hurt God, aimed instead at hurting His beloved creatures.

When the Creator announced to Satan, "I will put enmity between you and the woman," [30] He could have said, "I will put enmity between you and my Son." He clearly did

---

28 Fr. Rene Laurentin *El Demonio ¿Símbolo o Realidad?* Desclée de Brower, Bilbao, Spain.1998 p. 71.
29 John 19: 30.
30 Book of Genesis 3: 15.

not. Why? Saint Louis de Montfort had a deep understanding of why the Triune God had chosen Mary, His humblest creature, to be the one to fight the final battle against the enemy of His Creation. "Satan, being proud, suffers infinitely more from being beaten and punished by the little and humble handmaid of God (Mary), and her humility humbles him more than the Divine power." [31]

The Woman and the Spiritual
Battle of the Creatures

In His infinite Wisdom, God knows that Satan's greatest weakness is his pride, and that although he anticipates his unavoidable final defeat, he would have preferred to be defeated by the Son of God Himself. In his sick pride, that would turn his final defeat into *a victory*. If the *Son of God* had destroyed Satan during his saving mission on earth, the proud angel could have boasted

Image over the Basilica of Fátima

eternally that *it took the intervention of God himself to defeat him.* God is wiser than an arrogant evil angel. Since the existence of the poor demon depends solely on the Will of God, the Infinite Wisdom of the Creator anticipated that it did not require the intervention of the Son of God, to defeat a proud and disobedient angel. Although only the loving sacrifice of the Son of God could break the power of death over us and restore our friendship to the Father, His Divine hands did not need be soiled in a personal battle to defeat the evil creature.

So the Creator chose that this tremendous battle should be *a battle of creatures.* The spiritual Battle would be waged between the *proudest creature* and his evil followers against the *most humble of all creatures*, the Blessed Virgin and her consecrated souls. Due to his sick pride, such defeat humbles him more than a defeat by the Divine power. Could any Christian disagree with such Divine Logic?

This battle is also a call to humility for all of us pride-stricken creatures.

---

31 St. Louis De Montfort, *True Devotion To Mary* # 52.

It is much easier for us conceited creatures to "rally behind the Son of God" than it is to humbly pray the Rosary and rally behind another creature. It is easier for our ego to "go straight to Jesus" than it is to go and plead for the intercession of his humble Mother. The divine test of humility is perfect!

A Test of Obedience and Humility for Us, Creatures

The Book of Joshua reveals to us how the Creator requested the Israelite people to march meekly behind the Ark of the Old Covenant around the enemy walls of Jericho before He would grant them a great miraculous victory over the enemy. We can wonder why.

It was a divine test of obedience and humility. Before the eyes of the world, marching and entrusting their victory to a fancy decorated wooden box must have been perceived by the Israelites as embarrassing and humiliating. Why march behind a box when they could have gone straight to God? It was a tough test to their pride! They obediently did it, however, and God rewarded their humility with a victory over the enemy.

Since the Fall, we have all been exposed to and somewhat infected by the virus of pride disseminated by the Fallen Angel. We have a tendency to the sin of pride, so our loving God gives us the same opportunity that He once gave the Israelites against Jericho. This wise Divine Father, in His infinite mercy, designed a test that not only corrects, but also heals us.

Now, here is where the mission assigned to Our Lady comes into play. God knows that it would take true humility for us proud creatures to line up and march behind a human handmaiden, in order to bring down the walls of sin that separate us from our Creator. It would probably take as much humility and trust as it took for the Israelites to line up and march behind a wooden Ark before the mocking enemy crowds of Jericho. As we know, God was very pleased with their childlike humility.

God could have chosen numerous other ways to bring down the walls of Jericho. Ways more "dignifying" and pleasing to the egos of the Israelites than marching for seven days behind the Ark of the Covenant. This request, without a doubt, would seem ridiculous to an ignorant bystander but God did not chose the more "dignifying" way but the one that required more obedience and humility on the part of His children. Why? He was healing them from pride.

When our Lord asks us, the children of His Church, to march into the final spiritual battle behind the Ark of The New Covenant, He is not choosing the most "dignifying" manner of defeating the evil angel in the eyes of the wise but in those of the childlike faithful. Our Lord told us, "I give you praise, Father, Lord of heaven and earth, for although you have hidden these things from the wise and the learned you have revealed them to the childlike. Yes, Father, such has been your gracious will." [32]

How can a God Who will always keep His word, authorize the final battle between the prince of this world and the Queen of the angels in a world in which His human children have surrendered all jurisdiction to His enemy? Our Lady reminds us that *prayer is a condition willed by God, and the more insistently and the more often prayers are made, the more powerfully He will allow Our Lady to come with the holy angels to the aid of the Church.*

What is an act of Consecration?
Why do we need one?

God's children are being called to reverse this surrendering of the world once "entrusted" to them. How? As the time for the final battle approaches, the answer comes. In Fátima, right after the vision of hell, Our Lady gives us the condition: **God wishes to establish in the world devotion to my Immaculate Heart. If what I say to you is done, many souls will be saved and there will be peace.** The condition willed by God had been

---

32 (Luke 10: 21).

given. If the children respond, they would be spiritually prepared for the final climax of the battle of the creatures. How was this to be done?

During the apparition of June 13, 1929, to Sister Lucia at her convent in Tuy, Spain, Our Lady said: *The moment has come in which God asks the Holy Father, in union with all the bishops of the world, to make the consecration of Russia to my Immaculate Heart, promising to save it by this means...I have come to ask for reparation: sacrifice yourselves and pray.* The battleground is ready. God waits for those creatures to whom He gave jurisdiction to ask for His intercession through the consecration of the world once entrusted to man. God will not intervene personally. His favorite Daughter will do it!

Consecration: The voluntary act of entrusting and surrendering to God (or to Our Lady) our human jurisdiction over a person, a place or a thing.

God gave Man "dominion" over all the earth. At the fall, Adam, representing humanity, surrendered his jurisdiction over the world to the devil, whom Our Lord then called, "the Prince of this world."

God will not force His love on His creatures nor send His favorite humble daughter, Our Lady, to intervene, where she is not invoked nor appreciated.

Through an act of consecration to Our Lady, we attempt to revoke this satanic power, by willfully entrusting to Our Lady's protection and Queenly dominion that person, place or thing, over which Satan once laid claim. This then gives God just cause to allow Our Lady to come with the armies of Heavenly angels and intervene in our behalf.

In his first visit to Fátima, John Paul II explained the meaning of Consecration to the Immaculate Heart in his own words:

> *Consecrating the world to the Immaculate Heart of Mary means drawing near, through the Mother's intercession, to the fountain of life that sprang from Golgotha... Consecrating the world to the Immaculate Heart of the Mother means returning beneath the cross of the Son, it means consecrating this world to the pierced heart of the Savior, bringing it back to the very source of its redemption...The heart of the mother is aware of this, more*

than any other heart in the whole universe, visible and invisible. Consecrating ourselves to Mary means accepting her help to offer ourselves and the whole of mankind to Him who is holy, infinitely holy; it means accepting her help – by having recourse to her motherly heart, which beneath the cross was opened for every human being, mankind as a whole, and all the nations to Him who is infinitely holy.[33]

Consecration or Entrustment?

There has been some concern about the use of the word *consecration* for any other purpose than that of the sacraments, suggesting the use of

the word *entrustment* as a more suitable term. Yet, Our Lady did use the term consecration, and she knows better than anyone our God's desires. Our Holy Father explained at Fátima that there is no contradiction in the use of either term.

The Mother of Christ calls us, invites us to join with the Church of the living God in the consecration of the world, in this act of entrusting in which the world, mankind as a whole, the nations and each individual person are presented to the Eternal Father with the power of the redemption won by Christ.[34]

Sacred Heart at the Convent of Coimbra

---

33 John Paul II, Papal homily given May 13, 1982 at Fátima.
34 Ibid.

The Mystery of the Immaculate Heart and its Connection with the Rosary

FROM BETHLEHEM TO FÁTIMA

So, what is the mystery of the Immaculate Heart? What important role does it have for our spirituality and our salvation? Why is it so vital to the Message of Fátima for us? Someone foreign to Catholicism, may even ask, "Where is this devotion in the Bible?"

Let us realize that the first one to make mention of the *Heart of Our Lady* was Saint Luke himself: After the birth of Our Lord he tells us that "The shepherds went in haste and found Mary and Joseph, and the infant lying in the manger. When they saw this, they made known the message that had been told them about this child. All who heard it were amazed by what had been told them by the shepherds. And <u>Mary kept all these things, pondering on them in her heart</u>."[35]

Later, after the finding of Our Lord in the Jerusalem temple, Saint Luke added, "And he went down with them and came to Nazareth, and was obedient to them; <u>and his mother kept all these things in her heart</u>."[36] It is not difficult to believe that during the remaining sixteen years of their private life, Our Lord revealed to his Mother many more divine mysteries, which she also treasured and kept in her Immaculate Heart.

What is Saint Luke revealing to us? We could say that the maternal Heart of Mary is like the *Divine diary* in which God chose to record the amazing mysteries of Jesus' life on earth. Now by inviting us into the Immaculate Heart of His Mother, Jesus wants us to share in the amazing truths that He once revealed to her, but only if we are humble enough to go

---

35 Luke 2: 16-19.
36 Luke 2: 51.

to her through the mysteries of the Rosary!

The Rosary invites us to ponder the events of Our Lord's life in the company of His Divine Mother. It is like glancing at the pictures of a Mother's photo album of her Son's life, while she shares the insights of each picture! By meditating on His life, through her eyes, she gradually opens the hearts of her human children to contemplate the amazing mysteries that otherwise remain unreachable for us. Saint Luke also reveals this through the words of Simeon at the Presentation, "And a sword will pierce through your own soul also, <u>so that the thoughts of many hearts may be revealed</u>. Our Lady had to accept tremendous sufferings so that *our hearts could be opened.*

"On the cross Christ said 'Woman, behold your son!' With these words he opened in a new way his mother's heart. The Immaculate Heart of Mary, opened with these words, is spiritually united with the heart of her Son opened by the soldier's spear. Mary's heart was opened by the same love for man and for the world with which Christ loved man and the world... The power of the redemption is infinitely superior to the whole range of evil in man and the world. The heart of the mother is aware of this, more than any other heart in the whole universe, visible and invisible. And so she calls us. She not only calls us to be converted: she calls us to accept her motherly help to return to the source of redemption." (John Paul II, Papal homily, May 13, 1982, Fátima)

This is the supernatural gift that Our Lady is offering us at Fátima. She is inviting us into that special place, where all the amazing mysteries of her Son's life are stored, her Immaculate Heart! How can we possibly refuse such a priceless offering?

4

Portugal and the Biblical Meaning of a Crown

Do we know the essential difference between a king and an elected ruler? What is the actual difference between being a voter and being a subject?

This short segment is not a deep study on the *Theology of Government*, but merely some reflections to enlighten our Western mentality with a better comprehension of the royal monarchy and its implications in order to better comprehend what has taken place at Fátima. In the western world we celebrate "May crowning" devotions and we honor Our Lady with titles such as "Queen," but do we truly understand what such a title means before God? Do we understand the profound implications of recognizing someone as our "King", or our "Queen"? Do we realize the serious commitment that we make when we place a crown on Our Lady's head?

What is the True Meaning of a Crown?

The deeper dimension of the Message of Heaven in Fátima seems to be strongly connected with the monarchy. Understanding the role that monarchy seems to have in God's eyes is often something new and difficult for a westerner, since most of us have always lived under a democratic system. Kings have always been movie characters for us. Before we can understand and fully appreciate the role of Portugal in God's plan, we first have to understand their belief in and respect for royalty. In the present day, when the world

Monument to King Alfonso of Portugal

struggles with the concept of obedience to authority figures, the notion of a royal monarchy is very poorly grasped.

In the western world we grow up with a "fairytale" concept of princes and kings. This sometimes affects our understanding of the Queenship of Our Lady. Placing a crown of flowers over her image implies more than a mere act of pious affection. When you proclaim someone your "Queen", you are accepting your own role as a subject. Do we truly understand such a role before God? The power of a legitimate king or queen does not come from a human vote, it is granted from above!

In the beginning, God Himself reigned over Israel in virtue of the Covenant, but no human king incarnated His presence in the midst of his people.[37] Abraham, Moses, Joshua and Samuel were only *spokesmen* through whom God spoke and ruled His people. As spokesmen, they knew their limits. Each one would pass on to the people what God had commanded and nothing more. God led His beloved people through a representative on earth. It is interesting that in the present time there is only one nation

on earth that still follows this form of government - the Vatican City State and the Roman Catholic Church! Its authority is not the result of a human election, it comes from above. Although the Pope is elected at a conclave, his assignment comes through the inspiration of the Holy Spirit. God still leads His people through a representative on earth.

With God as their King, Israel could have become the most powerful and influential nation on earth, but the pride of the chosen children changed all this. They became tired

Crowned Image of the Queen of Portugal

37 King, *Dictionary of Biblical Theology*, Desclee Company, Belgium 1967. Page 251.

of having the Creator of the Universe for their personal king and demanded to be given an earthly king. In the book of Samuel we witness that the people came to God's prophet and demanded, "appoint for us a king to govern us like all the nations." (1 Samuel 8: 5) Until then, God had selected Israel to be an *example* to the other nations, but they were not interested. They preferred to become "like the other nations." We also hear the words of a rejected Father when the prophet informs Him of the people's request: "Appoint for us a king to govern us like all the nations."

The Loving Creator instructed the prophet to warn His Israelite children of the consequences of having another imperfect creature for a ruler:

> *These will be the ways of the king who will reign over you: he will take your sons and appoint them to his chariots and to be his horsemen, and to run before his chariots; and he will appoint for himself commanders of thousands and commanders of fifties, and some to plow his ground and to reap his harvest, and to make his implements of war and the equipment of his chariots. He will take your daughters to be perfumers and cooks and bakers. He will take the best of your fields and vineyards and olive orchards and give them to his servants. He will take the tenth of your grain and of your vineyards and give it to his officers and to his servants. He will take your menservants and maidservants, and the best of your cattle and your asses, and put them to his work. He will take the tenth of your flocks, and you shall be his slaves. And in that day you will cry out because of your king, whom you have chosen for yourselves; but the Lord will not answer you in that day.* (1 Samuel 8: 11)

His stubborn children, however, insisted, "No! but we will have a king over us, that we also may be like all the nations." After warning them about the dangers of having another imperfect creature for a ruler, God agreed to grant his children's request and gave them a human king: Saul. The rejected Creator told Samuel:

> *Hearken to the voice of the people in all that they say to you; for they have not rejected you, but they have rejected Me from being king over them. According to all the deeds, which they have done to Me, from the day I brought them up out of Egypt even to*

this day, forsaking Me and serving other gods, [38]

What a trade-off! They traded the most perfect and just King for another imperfect creature like themselves! God's children had taken the crown away from their Creator, and He had respected their free will. We must ask ourselves, when will the world return the crown to its Rightful Owner? The answer could be in the Message of Fatima!

The Creator Agreed to Give Man an Earthly King

Charlemagne's crowning by Leo III in 800AD

From this point on, we see a rejected but loving Father and Creator sending his prophets to anoint the kings and to remind them of ruling the people with fairness, and warning them against imitating the evil ways of the pagan kings.[39]

As we will discover with the history of Portugal, not all monarchs in history have been unjust rulers. Through the centuries numerous monarchs recognized that their royalty was a God-given birthright. In biblical times kings were usually anointed by a prophet of God, confirming their appointment. In the Middle Ages, numerous kings in Portugal and the rest of Europe requested the Pope or a bishop to be present at their crowning as a sign of their recognition of a higher power.

This is a historical declaration of early Portuguese kings about their royal authority as a God-given responsibility: "The just king truly lives up to his title, and preserves, for a long time his royal estate and dominion... so that he may rule his kingdom justly, and rightly and justly maintain

---

38 Samuel 8: 7-9.
39 Deut 17:14-20.

his people. And when he does not rule his people justly, then he does not merit being called a king. The first and principal virtue that is most fitting for a king or prince to have is justice, and this is so because it is a heavenly thing, one sent from God from His high heaven to the kings and princes of this world in order that they may be obliged to reign justly." [40]

A Lesson from the Portuguese

Our life in this world is a preparation for our eternal existence, and we are being prepared for a Kingdom. The New Testament message announces the coming of a Kingdom, *not of this world.*[41] **How does all this connect with the Message of Fátima?** Our Lady has already been anointed Queen by her Divine Son, but if we do not understand the seriousness of a crown, we will never fully understand the seriousness of a Consecration. Proclaiming someone as our king or Queen carries serious implications. God is not impressed by superficial crowning rituals. We should never proclaim anyone as our Queen, unless we are truly prepared to recognize ourselves as subjects.

The Tomb of King Pedro

40 *Afonsine Ordenaçoes* (royal ordinances) Fátima in the Light of History, by Costa Brochado. Bruce Publishing Co. MI 1955. Page 4.
41 John 18: 36.

As we are about to discover, in a wonderful way, in Fatima, Our Lord is calling us to recognize the Queenship He has granted to His Mother. Are our hearts truly ready for this? Now we return to the exciting history of Portugal. If to save the world God required an act of consecration, why did He choose the little country of Portugal? The Portuguese have already proclaimed the Queen of Heaven officially as their queen. Maybe the faithful humble deeds of an amazing Portuguese king will help us to answer this question.

5

Portugal: A Country with a Queen!

Why did Our Lady choose Portugal? The answer to this question could come only through the study of the history of Portugal in greater detail. I prayed about this for many years, then, during a recent visit to Fátima, the answer finally came. A faithful friend, a native of Fátima, posed this question while admiring a crowned image that we had purchased during a pilgrimage in Fátima. He asked us "Do you know why Our Lady wears a crown in Portugal." Puzzled by the question, I shook my head and he continued. "It is because Our Lady is the Queen of Portugal." At first we perceived his words as a mere statement triggered by devotion, but soon I realized we were in for a surprise!

Our encounter with this pilgrim was the trigger that led me to investigate further, and shortly Providence led me to literature dealing with that area of Portuguese history. In my study, I discovered a beautiful mystery that has remained pretty much unknown to the rest of the world.

According to these historical documents, my Portuguese friend's statement was based on an amazing historical fact. One that makes very obvious Our Lord's respect for the jurisdiction over the world that he had entrusted to man.

The nation of Portugal is situated in the Iberian Peninsula where devotion to the Immaculate Conception has existed at least since the Council of Toledo in 656 AD. From the beginning of the history of Portugal many rulers have invoked the intercession and protection of Our Lady for the land of Portugal. King João IV was not the first Portuguese monarch who placed the kingdom of Portugal under the protection of the Virgin Mary.

The first monarch of Portugal, King Alfonso Henriques, was himself miraculously cured from a disorder to his legs at the age of five,[42] awakening in him a lifetime Marian devotion. Later, King João I, in a sign of gratitude

---

42 *"Monarquia Lusitana"*, Fray António Brandão, 3ª parte, livro XI. Lisboa.

King Joao IV "The Restorer"

to Our Lady, placed on the doors of the capital a dedication praising the Virgin, and erected the monumental monastery of *Our Lady of the Battle (Nossa Senhora da Batalha)* in honor of Our Lady.[43] It was his successor King João IV, who, encouraged by the Franciscan and the Jesuit orders of his time, through an amazing royal decree made permanent the wonderful Marian devotion that Portuguese kings would frequently cling to at critical moments for their native land.

According to historical books, it all goes back to 1646, with the humble devotion of a king named João IV. He was a nobleman and the eighth Duke of the line of Bragança who, aided by Heavenly intervention, saved Portugal from being wiped out as a nation in the mid 1600's. The House of the Dukes of Bragança had a history of familial devotion to Our Lady of the Conception. In the early morning of December 1st of 1640, João IV accepted the risk of being proclaimed King of Portugal at a time when his nation had lost its independence to neighboring Spain for over sixty years. His role was that of restoring Portugal to its former independent status. This gained him the title *O Restaurador.* (The Restorer)

This king was a fervent Catholic and had very special devotion to Our Lady. He lived in his palace in the Portuguese town of Vila Viçosa and was a true supporter of the arts and culture. He founded a school of music and contributed to the composition of magnificent Marian hymns such as a *Magnificat* in four voices and an *Ave Maris Stella* in honor of Our Lady.[44]

---

43 Manuel Amaral www.arqnet.pt/dicionario/nsconcpad.htm
44 *Manual do Peregrino de Vila Vicosa.* Regia Confraria e da Confraria dos Escravos de Nossa Senhora de Conceiçao 2002. Vila Viçosa page 134.

The Portuguese King Calls on the Queen of Heaven

One of the king's first measures towards entrusting his nation to the protection of Our Lady, was to send a royal decree to the famous Portuguese University of Coimbra. The King commanded that all the students of the University of Coimbra, before taking any degree, should swear to defend the Immaculate Conception of the Mother of God.[45] The famous university complied. (After this, no one was ever admitted to academic degrees without taking such an oath, until it was considered no longer necessary due to the official definition of the Dogma of the Immaculate Conception by the Catholic Church.)

However, this was only the beginning. The King's devoted zeal was calling for the entrustment of the whole kingdom. He then announced that he had "resolved and ordained ... that all the cities, villages, and places in his kingdom's domains should take the Virgin, Our Lady of the Conception for Patroness."[46] At this point, the King encountered a requirement set by the "Congregation of Rites", which demanded that the election of a "Patron" or "Patroness" should initiate from an election and desire of the people. Between December of 1645 and March of 1646, the proposal was brought before the representatives of the Three States of the government, and was well received.

The King had official letters sent to all his subjects and his rulers over all the Portuguese territories (including Brazil) informing them of his intentions. After gaining their support, he officially made the most amazing declaration. For this wonderful ceremony he chose the *Feast of the Annunciation*, March 25th of 1646. (Curiously, 338 years later, Pope John Paul II would choose the very same feast-day to consecrate the whole world to the Immaculate Heart of Mary.) What inspired this humble

45 *A Virgem Maria Padroira e Rainha de Portugal.* Simão Pedro de Aguiã, Livraria Civilização Editora. Page 102.

46 *O Mysterio da Immaculade Conceição e a Universidade de Coimbra*, Dr. António Garcia Ribeiro, Page 92. Coimbra 1904.

King to choose such a date for his proclamation?

Finally, at the royal courts celebrated in Lisbon in March of the year 1646, and in the presence of all his Portuguese nobility and the Prince Elect, King João IV declared that he was officially taking the Virgin, "Our Lady of the Conception"[47] as Patroness of the Kingdom of Portugal. He promised to her in his own name, and in that of all his successors, the yearly tribute of 50 crusados[48] of gold.

The words of the proclamation chosen by the King were such that they were practically impossible to reverse. The proclamation even included a curse from God on any of his successors who would ever attempt to reverse this royal oath.

Royal Proclamation of King João IV on Our Lady's Queenship

I, King João, by the Grace of God, King of Portugal and of the Algarves (...), make known to all those who take notice of this proviso that, having now been restored by a very particular mercy of the Lord Our God, to the crown of these my kingdoms and lands of Portugal; and taking into account that the lord King Alfonso Henriques, my predecessor and first King of this kingdom, who upon being acclaimed and elevated as King, in acknowledgement of such a great mercy (...) took as his special advocate the Virgin Mother of God, Our Lady. And under her sacred protection and assistance he entrusted all of his successors, the kingdom and subjects with a particular tribute as a sign of subjection and servitude.

I, wishing to imitate his saintly zeal and the singular piety of

---

47 This an old Portuguese title for (Our Lady of) the Immaculate Conception: *Nossa Senhora da Imaculada Conceição.*

48 Also, "Cruzado"; English: "Crossed." It was a former coin of Portugal, made of gold or silver, displaying an image of a cross.

all my royal predecessors, (…) being now gathered in the courts with the three states of the kingdom, have made manifest to them the obligation we have to renew and continue this promise and to venerate with much particular affection and solemnity the feast of her Immaculate Conception; and in the courts, with approval from everybody, we have assented to take as Patroness of our kingdoms and colonies the Most Holy Virgin Our Lady of the Conception, (…) binding myself to procure the confirmation of the Holy Apostolic See, and I offer her again in my name, that of the Prince (…) my son, of all heir-successors, my Kingdoms, colonies and subjects, to her Holy House of the Conception located in Vila Viçosa, … fifty gold crusados per year, as a tribute of our vassalage.

And in the same manner, we promise and swear, along with the Prince and the Estates, to confess and defend always (to the point of giving up our life if necessary) that the Virgin Mary Mother of God was conceived without original sin; with great respect to the fact that the Holy Mother Roman Church, whom we are obliged to follow and obey, celebrates with a particular office the feast of her Most Holy and Immaculate Conception (…) trusting with great confidence in the infinite mercy of God our Lord, that by means of this Lady Patroness and Protectress of our Kingdoms and Lordships; of Whom we have the honor of confessing and recognizing ourselves as vassals and tributaries; may assist us and defend us from our enemies, with great increases of these kingdoms, for the glory of Christ our God, the exaltation of our Holy Roman Catholic Faith, the conversion of the peoples and the reduction of heretics.

And if any person should attempt to do anything contrary to our promise, our oath and our vassalage, being himself a servant, may he himself be declared as going against nature and may he be then cast out of the kingdom. And if it were the king (may God forbid), may he then make his our curse and may he no longer be counted among our successors, expecting that by the same God that gave us the kingdom and raised us to royal dignity, that he may be stripped and deposed by Him. Furthermore, so that our decision, promise and oath, made and established in the courts, may be certified for all time, We order that three solemn public acts be written. One of them will be promptly taken to the Court in Rome so that the confirmation of the Apostolic Holy See may be issued. And two more are to be kept in the archives of the House of Our Lady of the Conception in Vila Viçosa and in the Tower of Tombo, along with the above mentioned confirmation and with this provision of mine.

Given in this City of Lisbon on the twenty fifth day of March; through the writer Luis Teixeira from Cavalho in the year of Our Lord Jesus Christ, 1646, The King"

Lisbon, 25th of March of 1646 [49]

(Translated from Ancient Portuguese)

The king yet commanded that a carved stone tablet was to be placed at the gate of every city and village of Portugal. The inscription was to read: "It is true that with such a Protectress we can surely expect not only continuous victories over our enemies, but also great prosperity for our kingdom." [50] Such inscription varied in certain cities. In Leiria, one tablet still exists which reads: "The King of Portugal, Joao IV in union with the general courts officially consecrated himself and all his tributary domains of an annual census to the most pure conception of Mary. He signed an oath to always defend that the Mother of Jesus, chosen as Patroness of the Kingdom, was prevented from Original Sin. And, so that the faith of the Portuguese people may never give way, he ordered to have carved on living stone this perpetual memorial, in the years of the Lord, sixteen hundred and forty six, the sixth year of his reign." [51]

How could our God ignore such an act of humble submission? From that day on, the Portuguese are proud and fortunate to have

49   The dogma of the Immaculate Conception was not defined until the 8th of December of 1854 by Pope Pius IX by the papal bull *Ineffabilis*. (208 years after King Joao's proclamation!)

50   Silva Resende, *Nos Temos uma Rainha* Indugrafica Lda. - Fatima Leiria 1996 p.39

51   Silva Resende, *Nos Temos uma Rainha* Indugrafica Lda. - Fatima Leiria 1996   p.40

Our Lady of the Conception as their Patroness and Queen and nourish for Her a devotion that goes back to the beginning of the nation. Curious too is the fact that King João IV was making a solemn royal proclamation on behalf of Portugal, based on a belief that would not be declared an official dogma by the Church until 208 years later.

For some unexplained reason, the nation of Portugal has always shown a special devotion to the Immaculate Conception of Our Lady. Why so much emphasis on this particular Marian dogma? The other three Marian dogmas, the *Divine Maternity of Our Lady*, the *Perpetual Virginity* and the *Assumption*, have their foundation in the New Testament.

Its tremendous importance is found on the fact, that it is on this doctrine that the final battle between the Woman and the serpent is based. The battle against the devil can only be waged by a creature that has never been under his dominion of sin. To be the Woman "at enmity" with the devil, she had to be "the one creature" that never had any contact nor sinful dealings with him. The term *Immaculate Conception* means, that she never, not even at the moment of her conception, had her soul stained by sin. The Original

"King João IV taking off the royal crown and crowning Our Lady"

Sin of our first parents enslaves man, making Satan the temporary master of man. The Virgin was never under his sinful power. The Portuguese people have enthroned an Immaculate Queen.

Portuguese historians also report another amazing historical fact! On that date, in the Village of Vila Viçosa, King João IV (John IV), the royal monarch of Portugal, proclaimed Our Lady of the Conception[52] the Patroness of Portugal by removing the crown from his own head and crowning Our Lady's image as Queen.

An even more striking fact is that from that day on up to the present, no Portuguese monarch ever wore the crown. What an amazing proof of royal Marian devotion! Even some of the kings' wives refused to be referred to by the title "Queen of Portugal." Did this crowning of Our Lady have validity before God's eyes? We can be sure of that! God respects man's jurisdiction. The Portuguese king officially abdicated the crown of Portugal on our Lady's behalf. The Virgin Mary is officially the Queen of Portugal.

Did King João IV have the authority before God to speak for the subjects entrusted to him? Does God recognize the jurisdiction of a creature entrusted to rule over other creatures? Of course! Jesus, the God on earth, never required the personal consent of the centurion's dying servant (Matthew 8: 8-9) before accepting his master's intercession which saved him from death.

If God respects the jurisdiction of a Roman centurion over the men entrusted to him, how could he ever ignore the loving concern of a devoted Portuguese ruler over the nation of people entrusted to him? Obviously King João IV understood the accountability that came with his jurisdiction! He understood that it not only entails power but also responsibility. He used the authority and power entrusted to him, and he used it well. John Paul II once said: "The powerful must always remember that they owe their positions to God." [2]

King João IV entrusted his country to better and more powerful hands, those of the Queen of Heaven. If at the present time and since the murder of the last king in 1910, Portugal appears to be under a republican government, the faithful know better. Officially, and before God's eyes, they are a nation with a Queen!

---

52 This was the Portuguese title given to the *Immaculate Conception*. The term "Immaculate" was not officially added until years later.

2 Pope John Paul II's Visit to the United Nations and the United States, October 4th, 1995. Newark Cathedral

6

Fátima and its Amazing Role in World History

Another very little known dimension of Fátima is its amazing link with major historical events. Most faithful people seem to know that Our Lady of Fátima mentioned Russia during her apparitions, but for most, the rest of the actual details are very vague or little known. This brief segment is aimed to increase our insight of this historical dimension of Fátima. Let us look with a little more depth, and discover, what was Our Lady trying to prevent with her messages at Fátima? Why did she mention Russia?

Towards the end of the Nineteenth Century the anarchist movement was growing throughout Europe. The anarchists' philosophy of hate is to oppose all existing governments but especially monarchies. They hated private property and the ruling classes. They preached the necessity of violence, and recognized no moral absolutes. After the French Revolution, during the years 1894 to 1914, six heads of state were assassinated by the anarchists: the president of France, two prime ministers of Spain, Empress Elizabeth of Austria, the king of Italy, and President McKinley of the USA.[53] Sadly enough, the ruler of Russia, the Czar, was next.

Russia's Nightmare Begins

On the surface the Russian wealthy classes could believe that all was well and that their position was safe. Russia was considered one of the most religious and absolutist countries in Europe. The Russian Orthodox Church was very strong in the hearts of the Russian people and pilgrimages to holy Christian places were a major part of their lives. The Czar, Alexander II, respected by most, was seen as the ruler and unifier of all Russia. In most Russian homes a picture of the Czar hung near the icon of the Blessed Mother and the crucifix. Underneath, however, dark currents were

53 Anne W. Carroll, *Christ the King – Lord of History*. Tan Books. Rockford, Illinois 1994 p. 395.

Vladimir Lenin leader of the Soviets

growing, and the upper classes lacked the moral strength to deal with them.

Before the Twentieth Century began, Czar Alexander II had initiated many reforms to help his people, including the liberation of 48 million Russian serfs through an "Emancipation Act." In spite of these reforms that the Czar had put through, liberal revolutionaries hated him because they hated all authority. On March 1, 1881, they assassinated him while he was riding in his carriage.

Then Czar Alexander III came to power. He encouraged the industrialization of Russia. The liberals' plot to assassinate him too was uncovered and the conspirators were hanged. One of the assassins hanged had a brother by the name of Vladimir Lenin. Lenin read the communist teachings of Karl Marx and became a committed communist. In 1895, he stirred up workers' strikes and was sentenced to three years of exile in Siberia, during which time he and nine Marxists founded the *Russian Social Democrat Labor Party*. This was the dark beginning of the career of an evil man who would detrimentally change the history of the world forever.

Czar Nicholas II succeeded Alexander III. He was a good man who tried to do God's will but unfortunately was married to an interfering German princess named Alexandra. The royal couple had given life to four girls, but none of them could be the rightful

Russian Czar Nicholas II and his Family

heir to the Russian throne. Finally, in 1904, Alexandra gave birth to a hemophilic baby boy: Prince Alexis. As a result, Nicholas and Alexandra had to live in the shadow of their son's ill-health and the fear of any possible bruises that could kill him. It is about this time that appeared one of the strangest and darkest characters in history: a tall and bearded diabolical "monk" named Grigory Rasputin.

Rasputin was a corrupt man with a dominating personality and piercing eyes who seemed to exercise unexplainable supernatural powers. No one really knew what "religion" he held. Many witnesses had countless reasons to suppose that he was possessed. Unfortunately, the superstitious Queen Alexandra became convinced that Rasputin had been sent to them by God, and that he had supernatural powers to heal her son. Strangely, on a few occasions the evil man seemed to use certain strange

Grigory Rasputin 1917

preternatural powers that appeared to provide temporary relief to the ailing prince, thus strengthening his influence over the Queen. Although many feared him and disliked him, the Queen refused to believe the clear evidence of his immoral and promiscuous life. This assured Rasputin a place in the royal palace.

World War I began and the Russian general staff persuaded Czar Nicholas to respond with a general enlistment. This would have a fatal and detrimental future effect. The Czar became extremely distracted by the war. The situation in Russia went from bad to worse. While the Czar was away, Rasputin was left behind in the royal palace, by the Queen's side. Rasputin, supported by the superstitious Queen, continued to increase and exercise his evil power over the country and the people's respect for the royal family declined. The Russian people, including many aristocrats, could see the evil that Rasputin was doing to the nation, but Alexandra was blind to it.

Finally a group of loyal Russian aristocrats led by Felix Yusupov, afraid for the fate of their country, plotted to murder Rasputin. They hoped that, by assassinating this evil man, they could save Russia. His death is one of the strangest accounts in history. They poisoned him, shot him several times and beat him with clubs but were unable to kill him. This convinced them even further of his demonic involvement. Finally they finished by throwing him into a frozen river and drowning him.

On December 30, 1916 this demonic creature finally gave up the fight for his human existence, but it was too late; his diabolical mission had been accomplished. He had already sealed the fate and forever discredited the royal family in the eyes of the Russian people. The devil's evil attack against Russia had begun its course.

Russia and Fátima: What really took place in 1917?

The three little shepherds in 1917

The twentieth century was a century of light and darkness. It has been considered the cruelest of centuries, full of tribulations. Cardinal Sodano, while revealing the Third Secret, commented, "The vision of Fátima concerns above all the war waged by atheistic systems against the Church and Christians, and it describes the immense suffering endured by the witnesses of the faith in the last century of the second millennium. It is an interminable Way of the Cross led by the Popes of the twentieth century." [54]

Curiously, it appears that Satan's attack against the Church works on a schedule of one every two hundred years:

1517: On October 31, 1517, Fr. Martin Luther lit the spark which would trigger an irreparable separation throughout the "Church that Christ had built upon the Rock." On the church door in Wittenberg he nailed a document called the "Ninety-five Theses." Luther launched insults against the primacy of the Pope, the teaching authority of the Church,

54 Cardinal Sodano, *Announcement of Third Secret.* Fátima, May 13th, 2000.

the Holy Sacrifice of the Mass, and priestly celibacy. This caused millions of European Catholics to lose their faith and to leave the Church. Providentially, Our Lady responded by appearing in Mexico in 1531 and bringing about the mass conversion of more than nine million Mexican natives.

1717: On June 24, 1717 was founded the first Masonic Lodge in London, an international secret society. The Masons would later be the masterminds behind the bloody French Revolution that ended the monarchy in France, and under the name of the *Carbonarians* they claimed the credit behind the Portuguese Revolt, which assassinated the last Portuguese king and ended the monarchy in Portugal.[55] The Masonic Carbonarians then imposed a new constitution, which immediately proclaimed the "separation of Church and state" in Portugal, and elected Manuel Arriaga to the Presidency in 1911. He also was a well-known Mason.[56]

1917: In Russia, thanks to Rasputin's evil legacy, the reign of the Royal family came to an end, with the forced abdication of the Czar on March 15. Meanwhile, hiding like a serpent in Switzerland, after his Siberian exile, Vladimir Lenin was plotting. Lenin had conspired with the German government that if they could get him safely back to Russia he would take over the government and immediately withdraw Russia from the war. They transported him secretly in a sealed railway car.

Lenin arrived in Russia on April 16, 1917 and was welcomed by the ruthless Josef Stalin and a crowd of revolutionaries waving red banners. He immediately took charge of "the Bolsheviks", the most violent and radical of the revolutionary groups. As Lenin and the Bolsheviks secretly plotted the final destruction of freedom in Russia, loving eyes in Heaven were designing an alternate plan to help the world avoid the full magnitude of such a demonic scheme. This Divine plan was

1917: Lenin arriving on a train in Russia

55 The Carbonarians, www.citi.pt/cultura/literatura/poesia/j_g_ferreira/carbonar.html
56 *Fátima: Faith, Marvels, and Messages.* Inside The Vatican, August–September 1997, page 54.

to be declared in the nation of Portugal a month later in May of 1917.

It has been said that the Russian Revolution in 1917 was "the most important worldly event of the recent 20th Century", and "the Apparition of the Virgin Mary in Fátima, in 1917, was the most important Religious event of that century."[57] This continues to be true. Almost exactly one month after Lenin had secretly entered Russia, on April 16, 1917, the Blessed Virgin Mary responded by appearing in Fátima on May 13, 1917. Even after the recent changes in the former Soviet Union, both events continue to affect the world greatly in the present time.

It is also a fact that on May 5, 1917, Pope Benedict XV had offered a distressed prayer to the Blessed Virgin Mary, begging of her to bring peace to her children at war. Remarkably, eight days later, on May 13, 1917 the Virgin Mary, the Mother of God came to Portugal in person as an answer to the Pope's prayer. She appeared to three shepherd children in Portugal.

On July 8, 1917 the Russian army was totally wiped out, and Germany was able to send more divisions to the Western front. Back in Fátima, no one could have had access to this information. On July 13th, however, Our Lady predicted the end of World War I:

The War is going to end; but if people do not cease offending God, a worse one will break out during the pontificate of Pius XI…. To prevent this, I shall come to ask for the consecration of Russia to my Immaculate Heart, and the communion of reparation on the first Saturdays. If my requests are heeded, Russia will be converted, and there will be peace, if not she will spread her errors throughout the world, causing wars and persecutions of the Church. The good will be martyred, the Holy Father will have much to suffer, and various nations will be annihilated. In the end, my Immaculate Heart will

---

57 *Warren H Carrol,* Fátima. Video interviews with Ricardo Montalban. 1984.

triumph. The Holy Father will consecrate Russia to me, and she will be converted and a period of peace will be granted to the world...but in Portugal the Dogma of the faith will always be preserved.[58]

It should be pointed out, that at the time of Our Lady's prophecy in 1917 about Pius XI; no one had any way of knowing the official name that the future Pope would choose at his election in 1922. Only Heaven could know!

The tender innocence and limited education of the three little shepherds lends even more credibility to their testimony. Their lack of knowledge of world geography led them to believe that this *Russia* in Our Lady's message had to be "a very mean lady." Moreover, at the time of the apparitions, impoverished Russia was a menace to no one but the Russians themselves. Later on, the events demonstrated the actual connection.

On August 13, 1917, the children were unable to keep their appointment with the Lady at the *Cova de Iria* because the anti-Catholic magistrate had them arrested. He had attempted to scare them into denying that they were seeing the Mother of God. The children were threatened to be boiled in oil unless they admitted to be lying. Although frightened to death, the children did not concede. Finally, the frustrated magistrate released them. That month, the children did not see the Mother of God until the nineteenth of the same month. Meanwhile, back in Russia, Lenin continued his diabolical plot of death and destruction.

During October of 1917, the rains poured down all over Europe, on the soldiers wallowing in the muddy trenches of World War I, and on the thousands of pilgrims making their way to Fátima hoping to witness the

"How the Sun danced at noon in Fátima"
1917 Headlines

---

58   Sister Lucia's Memoirs, Secretariado dos Pastorinhos, Fátima, Portugal 2001.

promised miracle. On October 13, 1917, at Fátima, the rain ceased and Our Lady made her final apparition. During it, Our Lady spoke about the end of World War I, but the fate of Russia seemed to have already been sealed. After that, the sun danced and spun in the sky and appeared as if it were about to plummet to the earth. The children had been left with a heavenly message of repentance for the world, and a "Third secret" to be revealed only to the Pope.

Sadly, on November 7, 1917, what the Heavenly Lady had warned us about, began to happen: the final Russian revolution took place. The Bolsheviks, led by Lenin, seized the railroad stations, banks, power station, bridges and telephone exchange. Lenin was in control of "Mother Russia," one of the most religious Eastern European nations of the time. He ordered the seizure of all private property and took over all the Russian industry. He confiscated all church lands and said that divorce was legal and could be granted for any reason at all. Lenin conveniently re-instituted the death penalty and began to arrest his rivals. He went back on his promises to the people about a representative government. On June 12, 1918, he had the entire royal family of the Czar brutally murdered.

The Blessed Virgin's July prophecy was coming true. The evil of Communism had begun to spread its errors throughout the world, bringing untold suffering to millions of people, numerous wars and persecutions of Christians and of others as great as any the world has ever known. Finally on November 11, 1918, as she had predicted, World War I was over.

Our Lady's Prophesies about Russia come true

If my requests are not heeded Russia will
spread her errors throughout the world.

What were these errors to which our Lady was referring? One of the main ones was the diabolical philosophy of atheistic Communism. As we said before, Lenin received the bulk of his communist philosophy from reading the atheistic teachings of Karl Marx and Friedrich Engels in their *Communist Manifesto*. This malefic collection of writings has come to be known by many as the "Communist Bible." A great number of Catholics devoted to Mary admit having only a vague understanding of Communism. So in order to understand better what Our Lady of Fátima was trying to prevent, we, seeking the truth, should have a better understanding of this dark and infernal "philosophy."

It taught the following: First, that the history of humanity is that of a continuous class struggle. Society is divided into two groups, those who have wealth and those who do not. Secondly, it holds that the only way to achieve Communist goals is through violent destruction of the old order of society. The Communists believed that the time had come for the working classes to overthrow those in power and seize all power for themselves. Finally, it requires that law, morality and religion are to be rejected and eliminated. Thus, in whatever country Communism has been implemented, persecution of the Church and its clergy has been an essential requirement. In the *Communist Manifesto*, Marx advocated the abolishing of all religion.

Communism is essentially anti-religious since it sustains the diabolical position that religion must be totally rejected, because it was invented by those in power to suppress the poor and the weak. Its misinformation campaign spreads the message that belief in God makes people stupid and dull. Besides this, one of its prime strategies is the destruction of the people's sense of morality. One of its most constant strategic weapons is the promotion of immorality through the flooding of pornography. Thus, as can be expected, whatever country became the victim of a Communist invasion, witnessed the almost immediate bloody persecution of the Church and of the faithful who refused to give up their faith. Our Lady of Fátima knew the nightmare that was coming.

Some past skeptics question why Our Lady would deliver a political message against Communism. She did not. It is very doubtful that Heaven prefers one economic system to another for they all have their flaws. But

she knew that Communism and militant atheism go together. The philosophy of Communism requires organized and constant efforts to destroy religion and prevent religious worship and education. This is where it always encounters the denouncing voice of the Church. Our Lady was merely trying to prevent all the bloodshed and martyrdom that the spread of atheistic Communism was going to bring over the world.

The Communist Party under Lenin quickly tightened its grip on Russia, now renamed the Union of Soviet Socialist Republics, or the Soviet Union. Russian workers soon found out that the Communists had lied when they promised them a share in the ownership of factories, and went on strike. Due to a decline in manufacturing, in 1922, Lenin was forced to allow foreign investors in Russia. Unfortunately, before improvement could be felt, five million Russians died of starvation, proof of the inability of Communism to feed its people.[59] Millions of poor Russians found themselves experiencing "hell on earth." This is what the message at Fátima had tried to prevent!

...Causing Wars and Persecutions of the Church

Vladimir Lenin also hated religion. In Russia, as in the French Revolution, the religious instruction of children was prohibited. Religious books were banned. Numerous parochial schools, seminaries and monasteries were closed. Many bishops and priests were arrested and a lot of them were killed. The Russian Orthodox Church was forced to go underground in order to survive. This was a great blow to *Holy Mother Russia*, a nation once thought of as the most religious nation in the Eastern World. Once again, the Church was being called "to prevail" against another attack from hell.

Interestingly, Our Lady's six monthly apparitions in Fátima between May and October, took place between the time that Lenin entered Russia in April of 1917, and the time of the consummation of his evil plan in November of the same year. Could anyone call this a historical coincidence? It would take a lot of blind skepticism! Heaven's loving concern for us is a lot closer than what we realize. Our Lady is still trying to intervene in history and save us from our own mistakes but she cannot force us to listen.

---

59 Anne W. Carroll, *Christ the King – Lord of History*. Tan Books. Rockford, Illinois 1994, p. 419.

The Good will be Martyred,
...and Various Nations will be Annihilated

Young Karol Wojtyla

The spread of the errors of Russia did not take long. By 1920, the Soviet Union had marched and conquered the neighboring Christian country of the Ukraine, causing two man-made "famines" in which over eight million Ukrainians died. Later, Soviet armies were responsible for seven million more deaths. In 1921, Communist riots in Florence began a civil war in Italy, and in 1933, a Spanish Communist government began by attacking the Catholic Church. Many Spanish priests and nuns were murdered and many religious properties were confiscated and closed. In 1924, the religious name of the Russian capital was changed from *Saint Petersburg* (or Petrograd) to *Leningrad*, in honor of the dictator Lenin and as a symbol of its transition into a socialist city.

This was only the beginning of Satan's plan. In September of 1939, Russia joined Nazi Germany in invading the Catholic nation of Poland. The Communists then brutally murdered 10,000 Polish army officers. Luckily, Heaven was hiding a nineteen-year-old motherless Polish youth by the name of Karol Wojtyla from danger. In June 1940, the Soviet Union invaded and occupied the neighboring countries of Estonia, Latvia and the Catholic country of Lithuania. On June 27, they also occupied part of Rumania. Our Lady's prophetic, warning "...and various nations will be annihilated," was taking place, many nations were ceasing to exist.

In 1945, the Soviets established control over Hungary, Czechoslovakia, Yugoslavia, Rumania, and Bulgaria by brutality and terror. In August 1945, the Soviet Union declared war on Japan, and proceeded to seize Manchuria. After World War II, Winston Churchill and Franklin Roosevelt inhumanely granted Russia the permanent dominance over Poland, East Germany and North Korea. From North Korea, the Soviets poured military aid into communist China. In 1949, the Communists proclaimed the country the *People's Republic of China*. This Communist government, once in power, slaughtered hundreds of thousands, outlawed religion and brutally persecuted all Christians, natives and missionaries.[60] Can we envision the tears that fell from Heaven? Unfortunately, the spreading of errors still continued.

Providence allowed for Pope John Paul II to witness such horror as a young man, and he shares:

> *I have had personal experience of the reality of the "ideologies of evil." It is something that remains indelibly fixed in my memory. First there was Nazism. What we could see in those years was already something terrible enough. Yet many aspects of Nazism were still concealed at that stage. The real dimension of the evil that was unleashed in Europe was not perceived by everyone, not even by those among us who lived in the epicenter. We were totally swallowed up in a great eruption of evil (...). Both the Nazis during the War, and later the Communists in Eastern Europe tried to conceal what they were doing from public opinion. For a long time the West was unwilling to believe in the extermination of the Jews (...). Nor was it known in Poland all that the Nazis had done and were doing to Poles, or what the Soviets had done to the Polish officers in Katyn.[61]*

In 1950, the Soviets supplied Communist controlled North Korea with weapons and ammunition for the invasion of South Korea, triggering the Korean War and causing the death of over 7,500 American soldiers. In November of 1956, Hungarian freedom fighters heroically attempted to shake off the Communist yoke from their country. The Soviet Union sent Russian tanks into Hungary, leveling the capital city Budapest, executing hundreds of young Hungarians and sending thousands more to die in slave labor camps in Siberia, thus crushing the Hungarian hope for freedom. In January 1960, Catholic Cuba fell to the Communists, sending

60 Anne W. Carroll, *Christ the King – Lord of History*. Tan Books. Rockford, Illinois 1994, p. 450.
61 John Paul II, "Ideologies of Evil." Excerpts From his book *Memory and Identity*, Rizzoli Int. Publications, New York 2005, page 13.

thousands into exile. In 1964, however, Brazil was able to overthrow a pro-Communist government. A lady named Amelia Basto had organized a Rosary campaign in Brazil to save the country from a Communist takeover. She managed to recruit 600,000 women in 1962 to say the Rosary in Saõ Paulo for peace, and the country was spared a communist dictatorship by 1964. (Let us not forget that Brazil had been included in King João IV's proclamation of 1646.)

In 1975, the Communists launched a major attack against South Vietnam and soon had control of Laos and Cambodia as well. In Cambodia, the Communist government was responsible for the deaths of a quarter of the nation's population.[62] The Communists' only failure was in Portugal in 1975, where a massive opposition arose to a Communist government that had seized power and where on July 13, 1975, thousands of Portuguese people came to the Shrine of Fátima to beg their Queen's intercession for their country. By September, 1975, the Communists had been forced out of the government and Portugal was miraculously saved.

The purpose behind this painful historical segment is not to dwell morbidly on the bloody annihilation of so many unfortunate nations at the hands of Communism. Rather it is mentioned in order for us to remember that a great number of Marian devotees ignore and do not fully comprehend the deeper dimension of the message of Fátima and its historical consequences for our times. The Soviets murdered approximately 60 million human beings in half a century. Red China has murdered another 60 million. The Communists murdered one third of the Cambodian people in the 1970's.[63] It has been calculated that over 160 million casualties were victims of the atheistic system. Only by revisiting the bloody martyrdom of these nations and people can we come to realize the *real seriousness* of the Message of Our Lady at Fátima. Maybe the next time Our Lady pleads, the world will listen.

In the official commentary on the Third Secret by the Vatican, Cardinal Sodano explains:

> *Thus we come finally to the third part of the "secret" of Fátima which for the first time is being published in its entirety.... Let us now examine more closely the single images....At this point human persons appear: the Bishop dressed in white, other*

---

62 John Paul II, op cit., p. 458.
63 Fr. Robert Fox, *Fátima Today: The Third Millennium*, Park Press Quality Printing 2001, page 206.

Bishops, priests, men and women Religious, and men and women of different ranks and social positions. The Pope seems to precede the others, trembling and suffering because of all the horrors around him. Not only do the houses of the city lie half in ruins, but he makes his way among the corpses of the dead. The Church's path is thus described as a Via Crucis, as a journey through a time of violence, destruction and persecution. The history of an entire century can be seen represented in this image.... In the vision we can recognize the last century as a century of martyrs, a century of suffering and persecution for the Church, a century of World Wars and the many local wars which filled the last fifty years and have inflicted unprecedented forms of cruelty. In the "mirror" of this vision we see passing before us the witnesses of the faith decade by decade. Here it would be appropriate to mention a phrase from the letter which Sister Lucia wrote to the Holy Father on 12 May 1982: The third part of the "secret" refers to Our Lady's words: "If not, [Russia] will spread her errors throughout the world, causing wars and persecutions of the Church. The good will be martyred; the Holy Father will have much to suffer; various nations will be annihilated". [64]

This is the suffering that the Lady from Heaven came to prevent. But the world did not respond in time to her 1917 plea for prayer and sacrifice. Therefore, the world has suffered tremendously. In the presence of so much evil, an observer could easily fall into despair. Due to so many millions of deaths, many have called the Twentieth Century "the century of Satan." But there is hope! There is a mother's promise, also given in 1917, "In the end, my Immaculate Heart will triumph. The Holy Father will consecrate Russia to me, and she will be converted and a period of peace will be granted to the world." Thank God!

Our Lady of Fátima's Amazing Historical Response

In October 1978, Our Lady's response to Satan's scourge of the world begins to appear. A Polish Cardinal closely familiar with the Communist scourge was elected to the Chair of Peter. His name was Karol Wojtyla.

---

64 Fátima Secret-Message and Commentary, Congregation for the Doctrine of the Faith.

John Paul II arriving in Fátima

He humbly assumed the papal name of John Paul II, in honor of his predecessors, John XXIII, Paul VI and John Paul I. He was the first non-Italian pope in 455 years. As he was introduced to the world he greeted the faithful saying, "I have come from a faraway country!"

Yes, a country that had experienced a horrific scourge of suffering at the hands of Communism and had maintained the faith! No one could be better prepared by Our Lady to deal with internal aspects of Communism than was Pope John Paul II. He knew well the manipulative ways of Communism. As Cardinal of Poland, he had repeatedly dealt with the Communist authorities and had many positive results. It was reported that the Moscow Communist leaders were tremendously concerned with this unexpected move of the Holy Spirit. This former Polish archbishop was now the Pope!

The new Pope began to shake the Soviet Communist "stability" with several trips to countries behind the Communist iron curtain, including his native land, Poland. His influence soon became too great for comfort and what many experts call a "response" came. On May 13, 1981, in Rome, Pope John Paul II was shot in an assassination attempt in St. Peter's Square.

Although the Pope kept the assassin Mehemet Ali Agca's secret of who hired him, Agca later claimed to be part of a Communist conspiracy pressured by the KGB. They had ordered him to assassinate the Pope because of his support of Poland's Solidarity Movement.[65] Although nothing has been officially proven, it has been said that the KGB did not choose the wrong day to assassinate the Pope, they chose the wrong date!... the *anniversary of Fátima*

On May 13, 1982, Pope John Paul II traveled to Fátima to thank Our Lady for saving his life. He attempted to consecrate Russia. Later, from her convent Sister Lucia said that the attempt did not include the bishops' participation required by Mary. On March 25, 1984, back in Rome, Pope John Paul II, requested the bishops of the world to join him, and he renewed the consecration of the world to the Virgin Mary. This time Sister Lucia said that the conditions God required were *fulfilled* and that *God would keep his word.*

God soon began to fulfill Our Lady's prediction. Within two months of the consecration, on Sunday May 13, 1984, the Holy Father spoke to over 50,000 pilgrims in St. Peter's and called for a Rosary crusade because of the grave danger to world peace at that time. In compliance with his request, Marian organizations launched a major "Rosaries for peace" crusade. There was a wonderful response. On that very same day, one of the largest crowds in Fátima's history gathered at the Portuguese shrine to pray the Rosary for peace. Curiously, also on that very same day a mysterious explosion at the Soviets' Severomorsk Naval Base destroyed 80% of all the missiles stockpiled for the Soviets' Northern Fleet. The blast also destroyed the workshops needed to maintain the missiles as well as hundreds of scientists and technicians. Western military experts called it "the worst naval disaster the Soviet Navy had suffered since WWII."[66] God was keeping His Word.

In addition to these events, the Soviet Defense Minister assigned to be the mastermind behind the invasion plans, suddenly became seriously ill and then died in December of 1984. Four years later, during the Vigil for the Anniversary of May 13, 1988, as thousands prayed the Rosary at Fátima; another mysterious explosion wrecked the only factory that made the rocket motors for the Soviets' deadly SS 24 long-range missiles, which carry ten nuclear bombs each.[67] Finally, on December 1st 1989, in the Vatican, Soviet President Mikhail Gorbachev came to the Vatican and met

---

65 Italian Parliamentary Commission's Report., Zenit News Agency. March 7, 2006.
66 The Power of the Rosary. www.opusangelorum.org Formation/Holyrosary.html
67 Ibid.

with Pope John Paul II, breaking 70 decades of spiritual conflict, and promised religious freedom for the Soviet citizens.

Satan, however, was not going to give up easily, and on August 19, 1991, a group of Gorbachev's ministers, backed by the KGB and military, staged a coup. This was the anniversary of Our Lady's August apparition to the children (they had been arrested

Russian president Gorbachev visits the Pope at the Vatican

on the 13th of August 1917). Gorbachev was held prisoner in his summer residence, and martial law was declared in Russia. Large groups of soldiers controlled Moscow, but no politicians were arrested. This time success was not going to be theirs to enjoy. Once again, the Communists had chosen the wrong date! On the same day more than 100,000 Russian people, many praying the Rosary, rallied outside the Soviet Union's parliament building protesting the coup that had deposed Gorbachev. During this time, Estonia declared its independence (on August 20).

On August 21, Latvia, declared its independence. Finally, on August 22th, 1991, the Feast of the Queenship of Mary, the coup failed. Even before Mikhail Gorbachev returned to Moscow, Boris Yeltsin assumed power and immediately signed a decree banning the Communist party throughout Russia. The ban was soon extended throughout the Soviet Union. Thus 70 years of Communist rule effectively came to an end. The date could not be a coincidence. What a way to celebrate Our Lady's Queenship! On December 21, 1991 all the remaining republics (except Georgia) founded the *Commonwealth of Independent States*, ending the USSR. On Christmas Day 1991, Gorbachev resigned as president, and the USSR was officially dissolved! Gorbachev later said, "Everything that happened in Eastern Europe in these last few years would have been impossible without the presence of this pope." "The pope did everything possible to help humanity out of its era of hate."

On October 12 - 13, 1991, the anniversary of the Miracle of the Sun was celebrated in Fatima. The Catholic Archbishop from Moscow Tadeusz Kondrusiewicz, was there leading the first Russian pilgrimage group to Fátima. With tears of emotion, he officially thanked Our Lady of Fátima for the changes in Russia. The event was televised in Russia on 150 TV stations and 350 radio stations. Later, that same year on Christmas Day, the red Communist flag waved for the last time over Russia. Gone were the hammer and the sickle. On December 30, 1991 fifteen republics were freed from Soviet domination.

On May 13, 2007, the Archbishop of Moscow declared that during that first visit to Fátima, *I had also the opportunity of meeting with Sister Lúcia for the first time. She truly could not believe that the archbishop of Moscow had arrived. I recollect her words that, "the president of the USSR, Mr. Mikhail Gorbachev, is the instrument in the hands of God and that the mystery of Fátima was about to be realized."*[68]

On May 13, 2000, John Paul II returned to Fátima for a third time, bringing the attention of the Third Millennium back to the message of Fátima. Later that year, he would perform an act of unprecedented magnitude that would have unspeakable future outcome. He requested the Portuguese Bishop of Fátima, to have the famous image of Our Lady flown once more to the Vatican. This would be only the second time in history that the Shrine authorities permitted the precious image to leave

The Pope's arrival in Fátima for the Beatification

68 Interview realized by *LeopolDina Reis Simões*-Sala de Imprensa of the Social Communications Center of the Fátima Shrine. Bulletin May 19, 2007

Portugal.

What was so special that the John Paul II deemed it necessary to make such a request? This time it would be for the Jubilee Gathering of all the bishops of the world at the Vatican on October 8, 2000. What was in our Holy Father's mind? Once the blessed image was at the Vatican, the Pope led the world in the praying of the Rosary and invited all the bishops of the world to join him in an *Act of Entrustment* of the whole world and the Third Millennium to the Immaculate Heart of Mary. This time there would be no doubt regarding the participation of the bishops of the world. Each bishop received a copy of the *Act of Entrustment* in his own language. Nearly 1500 bishops present read it along with the Pope. Together they prayed in the Pope's words:

O Mother ...Today we wish to entrust to you the future that awaits us, and we ask you to be with us on our way. We are the men and women of an extraordinary time, exhilarating yet full of contradictions. Humanity now has instruments of unprecedented power: We can turn this world into a garden, or reduce it to a pile of rubble.... Today as never before in the past, humanity stands at a crossroads. And once again, O Virgin Most Holy, salvation lies fully and uniquely in Jesus, your Son.

Did the world realize what had taken place that day? This time there could be no misgivings! An official collegial act had been done. All the Catholic bishops of the world had been convoked to be there. All those present had joined the Holy Father. The Third Millennium has been officially entrusted to the Woman of the Apocalypse. Now the "Battle of the Millennium" could begin.

A Sign of Hope: Our Lady's Flag

Although Satan has never yet manifested his evil self in a red suit with a pitchfork, through the evil of Communism he tried to establish and mark his territories with the sign of the Red Flag. In the past seventy years, millions of Western and Eastern Europeans were forced to suffer bloodshed and atrocities under the symbol of the Soviet "Red Flag." Fortunately, God's sense of fairness reflects a bit of humorous irony. While the Communist Red Flag has ceased to oppress many tortured nations, another flag is foretelling a sign of hope.

European Flag: Blue with 12 gold stars

It is reported that on December 8, 1955, on the Catholic Feast of The Immaculate Conception of Mary, the European Ministers' delegates officially adopted the European flag, twelve stars on a blue background, designed by Mr. Arsene Heitz, who, today, is an octogenarian artist in Strasbourg. What was unknown to most of the ministers was the symbolism behind the flag.

A short time ago the artist, Mr. Heitz, a devotee of the Virgin Mary, revealed to a French publication the reason behind his inspiration. According to the artist himself, he thought of the twelve stars in a circle on a blue background, exactly the way it is represented in the traditional symbolism of the *Woman of the Apocalypse*. At that time he was reading the history of the Blessed Virgin's apparitions at *Rue du Bac*, in Paris. There, Our Lady

Soviet Communist Flag burning ceremony in Russia

made a request for a Miraculous Medal with a crown of 12 stars. [69]

A former Secretary-General of the Council of Europe, Leon Marchal, later affirmed that the stars are those of the *Woman of the Apocalypse*. The European Union, which on May 1, 2004 raised its number of member countries to twenty-five, has confirmed that the number of stars will always remain at twelve. Amazingly, eight of the last 10 nations to join the European Union, Latvia, Lithuania, Malta, Slovakia, Estonia, Hungary, Czech Republic, and Poland were former tortured nations under the Communist Red Flag.

---

69 "Coincidences" of European Flag. Zenit News Agency December 7, 1999 Archive. www.zenit.org/english

Although at the time of the flag's approval the artist's intent was not known to the members, the flag was approved. EU headquarters in Brussels, says: "The European flag (is) a shared flag, blue with twelve gold stars symbolizing completeness. The number will remain twelve no matter how many countries there are in the European Union." [70]

The secret behind the flag has become known all over Europe, making some devotees very happy, and some anti-clericals and atheists very uncomfortable. A well-known European Professor of contemporary history responded that no one had a reason to feel offended because, "neither the stars nor the blue of the flag are particularly religious symbols, thus respecting the conscience of all Europeans, regardless of their beliefs." [71]

Although certain anti-Catholic groups have attempted to deny or ridicule the symbolism behind the flag, the result is still a reality: While Hitler's red swastika flag and the red Soviet flag have come down from many poles; the Marian symbol of twelve stars is now on almost every license plate of the European Union and on every banknote in Europe. What a historical "twist of flags!" It seems that the Queen of the World is getting ready to reclaim her territories!

Vatican Euro Coin

But, this new economic union must avoid repeating errors from the past. Five months before his death, John Paul II gave his fatherly advice to the 25 government leaders in the European Union about the Christian role in the making of the continent: "The Holy See has reminded all that Christianity, in its different expressions, has contributed to the formation of a common conscience of European peoples and has helped enormously in shaping its civilizations. Whether or not it is recognized in official documents, it is an undeniable fact that no historian will be able to forget." [72] He added, "Therefore, I hope that also in the years to come, Christians will continue to contribute, in all ambits of European institutions, that evangelical ferment that is the guarantee of peace and collaboration among all citizens in the shared commitment to serve the common good,"[73] Will they listen this time?

70 *Mary's Stars on the European Flag* www.giveshare.org/BibleStudy/226.marysstars
71 Catholic Answers. "This Rock." www.catholic.com/thisrock/2000/0002drag.asp
72 Zenit News Organization. *"Pope Reiterates Christianity's Role in Making of Europe"* October 28, 2004.
73 Zenit News Organization. *"Pope Comments on the Signing of EU Constitutional Treaty"* October 31, 2004.

World War II and the
Fátima Prophecy of October 13ᵗʰ

Nazi invaders marching into Austria

At this point it seems necessary to recall another amazing Fátima prophecy that came to fulfillment in the previous century. In March of 1933, elections took place in Germany, and the Nazi party took a majority of the votes, bringing Adolph Hitler to power as chancellor. Hitler immediately ordered the arrest of 81 opposing communists and invoked the "Enabling Act" which gave him "the power to rule without consulting the German Parliament" and setting him as a dictator. Hitler manipulated the oath of allegiance taken by army officers. No longer would they swear allegiance to the nation of Germany but to Hitler personally.[74]

From the moment he took power in 1933, Adolph Hitler knew what he wanted. He would use any method necessary, no matter how immoral, in order to accomplish his plans. In 1937, Pope Pius XI wrote an encyclical called "Mit Brennender Sorge" ("With Burning Sorrow") condemning Nazism. Hitler stated that he would bring the rest of Europe under his control and then turn on his last and greatest Enemy: *the Catholic Church.*[75]

Hitler's first goal was to unite all the German-speaking peoples under his domination. His first target was Austria. In the absence of the Austrian Emperor Charles of Hapsburg, Hitler sent his troops to invade Austria on March 13, 1938.

---

74 Anne W. Carroll, *Christ the King – Lord of History.* Tan Books Rockford, Illinois 1994. p. 423.
75 Ibid., p. 423.

Photograph of the Aurora Borealis

Our Lady of Fátima and Her Prophecy about World War II

During her July 13th apparition, back in 1917, Our Lady predicted the end of World War I. Sadly, She had also made a prophetic warning: *If people do not cease offending God, a worse one will break out during the pontificate of Pius XI. When you see a night illumined by an unknown light, know that this is the great sign given you by God that he is about to punish the world for its crimes, by means of war.* On January 25th and

26th of 1938, an "unknown light" which many identified as the Aurora Borealis was seen all over Europe. Was this the light announced by Our Lady in Fátima, twenty years earlier?

Back in her Portuguese Convent in Coimbra, Sister Lucia witnessed from her window the strange light in the sky. She knew that this was the sign announcing that the prophecy was about to be fulfilled. Recognizing this, Sister Lucia wrote to the Cardinal Patriarch of Lisbon, informing him that war was imminent. Forty days later, on March 13, 1938 Hitler invaded Austria. This would prove to be the event that would set in motion a series of events which would cause the beginning of World War II in September of 1939. The prophecy of the Lady of Fátima had come true. As predicted, another war had begun during the reign of Pope Pius XI!

Within a year's time Hitler unleashed his bloodthirsty Nazi army on Europe and World War II had begun. He invaded Czechoslovakia, Poland, Denmark, Norway, Holland, France and eventually went after Russia. Curiously, the little country of Portugal was again providentially protected and kept out of the diabolical scourge of World War II. This country had a powerful Queen who shielded them!

7

Our Lady's Crowning and the Popes

Did King João IV's generous royal decree go unnoticed by the Church? Did it ever receive any recognition from the Holy See? In his proclamation, King João IV had ordered that one of his three "Public Acts" be "promptly taken to the Court in Rome." Twenty-five years after the 1646 ceremony, on May 8, 1671, Pope Clement X, in his brief letter *Eximia dilectissimi*, responded by confirming solemnly Our Lady's election as Patroness of Portugal.

On May 13 of 1946, on the Three-hundredth Anniversary of King Joao's Proclamation, the Papal Nuncio of Pope Pius XII, Cardinal Aloysius Masela, arrived in Fátima. The papal nuncio had orders from the Pope to crown Our Lady of Fátima, not only as "Queen of Portugal," but as "Queen of the World."

Pius XII's papal nuncio, Cardinal Aloysius Masela crowning Our Lady of Fátima in 1946

Reportedly, Our Lady's crown was a gift from numerous Portuguese humble women who decided to donate their wedding rings to be melted into a jeweled gold crown for their Queen. What a filial act! I once read the comments of some negative critics who perceived this as an act of excessive religious fervor on the part of these generous women. Let them consider what could be Heaven's perception of such a sign of love!

In the Sinai desert the Israelites donated all their golden jewelry to melt for themselves a pagan "golden calf", which deeply offended our

Gold Crown donated by Portuguese women after melting their wedding bands

Father and Creator. These humble Portuguese daughters donated their precious wedding bands to offer a crown to the Heavenly mother of their Lord as their Queen. On May 13, 2000, I witnessed the Holy Father joining himself to these women's generosity, when he offered and left his own precious ring at the feet of the image Our Lady of Fátima.

The crown of Our Lady weighed 1,200 grams and it was adorned with 313 pearls and over 2600 precious stones. From that day on, Our Lady's image at the Shrine wore the crown that one day would also hold the bullet that went through the Pope's body during the attempt on his life. During the 1946 coronation, Pius XII did not fail to mention of the King's actions exactly 300 years before (1646-1946). These are some of his beautiful words:

Three hundred years ago, the king of the (Portuguese) restoration, as a sign of his own and his people's love and appreciation, <u>placed the royal crown at the feet of the Immaculate, proclaiming her Queen and Patroness</u>. Today, all of you, the people of the Land of Holy Mary, together with the Shepherds of your souls, and its government, with the ardent prayers, the generous sacrifices, the eucharistic solemnities, and the thousand respects that your filial love and appreciation dictated to you. You assembled that precious crown and with it you girded the forehead of Our Lady of Fátima, here in this blessed oasis, impregnated with the supernatural, where one can more sensibly experience Her *prodigious patronage, where all of you feel closer her Immaculate heart beating with immense tenderness and maternal concern for you and the world.*[76]

The Indisputable Royalty of the Virgin Mary

Pius XII concluded his letter thus:

Jesus is the King of the Eternal Centuries by nature and by conquest. With Him and in subordination to Him, <u>Mary is Queen, by grace and by divine maternity, by conquest and by singular election</u>. Her kingdom is as vast as that of her Son and her God, since nothing was excluded from her domain. And it is for that reason that the Church honors her as Sovereign and Queen of the angels and the saints, of the patriarchs and the prophets, of the Apostles and the mar-

tyrs, of confessors and virgins. For this reason it proclaims her, the Queen of the Universe and teaches us to invoke her night and day in the midst of the mourning and weeping of this exile, "Hail Holy Queen, Mother of Mercy, our life, our sweetness and our Hope."[77]

"Fatima Shrine's Image before being officially crowned in 1946"

---

76 Pius XII, *Radiomensajem na coroaçao de Nossa Senhora de Fátima,* May 5, 1946. *Manual do Peregrino de Vila Viçosa,* 2002. page 37.

77 Ibid., p. 40.

**Pope Paul VI placing
Tiara on the Altar**

On the Anniversary day of Fátima, May 13, 1965, Pope Paul VI sent a Golden Rose to Fátima, confiding the entire Church to our Lady's protection and gave the official Church recognition of Fátima's significance for the universal Church. Two years later, on May 13, 1967, Pope Paul VI traveled to Portugal, and became the first Pope to go to Fátima as a pilgrim. While there he renewed the consecration to the Immaculate Heart of Mary.

Interestingly, Pope Paul VI, the first Pope to visit the Shrine of Fátima, was also the last pontiff to wear the Papal Tiara. The Tiara was a crown symbolizing the threefold authority of the Supreme Pontiff. It was decorated with three smaller diadems, signifying, the Pope's authority as Universal Pastor (top crown), his Universal Ecclesiastical Jurisdiction (middle crown) and Temporal Power (bottom crown). Of this last authority, only the Vatican City State remains from the papal territories which in past ages secured the autonomy of the Vicar of Christ from the princes and rulers of this world. [78]

At the end of the Second Vatican Council, Pope Paul VI descended the steps of the papal throne in St Peter's Basilica and laid the tiara on the altar in a dramatic gesture of humility and as a sign of the renunciation of human glory and power in keeping with the renewed spirit of the Second Vatican Council. This last tiara was then given to

Pope's Tiara

78 www.geocities.com/rexstupormundi/papalmonarchy.html

benefit the poor, but remains as a symbol in the papal crest. For hundreds of years each new Pope had taken office in a coronation ceremony. After the humble act by Paul VI, Pope John Paul I and John Paul II also declined this act as did their successor, Benedict XVI. Does this picture seem familiar?

John Paul II Recognizes the Proclamation of King João IV

One year after the attempt on his life, John Paul II arrived at Fátima on May 13, 1982, to thank Our Lady for saving his life:

And so I come here today because on this very day last year, in Saint Peter's Square in Rome, the attempt on the pope's life was made, in mysterious coincidence with the anniversary of the first apparition at Fátima, which occurred on May 13, 1917.

I seemed to recognize in the coincidence of the dates a special call to come to this place. And so, today I am here. I have come in order to thank Divine Providence in this place, which the Mother of God seems to have chosen in a particular way. "Through God's mercy we were spared". (John Paul II, Papal homily, May 13, 1982, Fátima)

The very next day, May 14, 1982, showing his aware-ness of the royal con-secration of 1646, John Paul II traveled south of Fátima, to the Portuguese Shrine of "Our Lady of the Conception" in Vila Viçosa. This is where King João IV had crowned our Lady in 1646. The Pope honored Our Lady and showed

**Church of Our Lady
of the Conception, Vila Vlçosa**

his endorsement of the King's Consecration. The Pope said:

> *Here in the Shrine of Our Lady of the Conception of Vila Viçosa, under the gaze of the Queen of Portugal, crowned by King João IV (...) Here, in this shrine of the Immaculate Virgin, today the Bishop of Rome and successor of Peter raises his hands, his thoughts and his heart together with all the sons and daughters of this Portuguese land.*[79]

The Portuguese faithful erected a historical monument with a bronze bust of the Holy Father, John Paul II, outside the little church inside of the Castle of Vila Viçosa in remembrance of the Pope's visit. Through this visit, John Paul II also recognized King João IV's authority and the seriousness of his actions. During the same visit to Portugal the Pope later added...

S.S. JOÃO PAULO II

PEREGRINO
DE
Nª SRª DA CONCEIÇÃO
PADROEIRA DE PORTUGAL

VILA VIÇOSA
14 DE MAIO DE 1982

**John Paul II,
Pilgrim to Vila Viçosa**

> *One day Portugal was the pulpit of the Good news of Jesus Christ for the world, which was carried far in fragile ships by heralds impelled by the breath of the Spirit. Today I come here too, to the same platform, to convoke all of the People of God for the evangelization of the world (...) that each one of you today become a daring witness of the Gospel of Jesus Christ, at the meeting of so many lives hungry for God:* **Portugal, I call you to a mission.**[80]

On October 13th of 1996, Cardinal Ratzinger, later Pope Benedict XVI, also visited Fátima. In his homily to the pilgrims he stated,

> *Through the two great signs of Lourdes and of Fátima, she is known,*

---

79 John Paul II, Vila Viçosa, Portugal. May 14, 1982, *Manual do Peregrino de Vila Viçosa*, 2002.
80 Ibid. (Manual's rear cover)

as Mother of Mercy and she exhorts us. She does not need too many words, because everything has been said, through those essential words of hers which are entirely impregnated with maternal request: "do whatever he tells you". We should also notice that Mary spoke to the small ones, to the minors, to those without voice, to the ones that do not count, in this enlightened world, full of pride of knowledge and of faith in the progress, which is, at the same time, a full world of destruction, full of fear and despair.

Monument to the three Little Shepherds at the
Place of the Angel

8

Portugal: A Country with a mission!

Recently, on May 13, 2001, the Shrine of Fátima had a very special visitor. It was the Duke Duarte de Bragança with his wife and children. He is the rightful heir of the Portuguese Royal family and successor of King João IV. Interestingly, born in exile, he also became the godson of Pope Pius XII. The Duke came to the Fátima shrine and delivered this Official public Communication:

Duke Duarte's family in the Pope's private library

I find myself in Fátima, together with my wife and children and united with you in prayer, on this day chosen by the Virgin Mary to visit the Portuguese people and all humanity.

Already my predecessor the king João IV, in union with all the representatives of the Portuguese people crowned the Virgin Mary as the Queen of Portugal, and ***up to the present day, no political regime has ever dared to withdraw the Crown of Portugal from Her.***

> *From this reality comes a tremendous responsibility for all of us Portuguese people, living in Portugal or disseminated around the world, where you represent with much courage, merit and dignity, the name of our nation.* (Official Royal Communicate)[81]

What a beautiful mandate! What a powerful reminder to the Portuguese people, of their responsibility for the mission entrusted to them! Regardless of the moderation of the Portuguese republican régime, there is still considerable sympathy for the monarchist cause. Many recognize that it was the monarchy which made it possible for Portugal to achieve and sustain its independence from Spain. It was also the Bragança Kings who advanced the country's commercial and trading relations.

Today, Duke Duarte is treated with enormous respect and his strong Marian devotion is not a secret. His recent wedding to a Portuguese noblewoman took place on the Fátima Anniversary of May 13, 1995! It was an occasion for national celebration. The ceremony received the kind of national television coverage that would be expected of a reigning monarch. Duke Duarte, after serving in the Portuguese Air Force, has dedicated himself to advancing the spread of Christianity, mainly in Russia where for many years he has sponsored the distribution of Bibles.[82] He is the Sovereign Grand Master of the Order of Our Lady of the Conception of Vila Viçosa, and Sovereign of the Royal Order of Saint Isabel. His wife, Her Royal Highness Isabel, Duchess of Bragança, is the "Grand Mistress" of the order. Their Royal Highnesses live in São Pedro de Sintra, near Lisbon.

Duke Duarte de Bragança
heir to the Portuguese throne

Duke Duarte was born in exile on May 15, 1945 in the Portuguese Embassy in Bern, Switzerland, due to the Law of Banishment then still in effect in Portugal. Upon the revocation of the Law of Banishment by the Portuguese Parliament in the 1950s, the Royal Family was presented with a residence in Portugal by the Fundação Casa de Bragança.

---

81 The Royal Communicate was published in www.reallisboa.pt/boletim/47_48/comunica.html

82 *The Order of Our Lady of The Conception of Vila Viçosa*, www.chivalricorders.org/orders/portugal/vilavic.htm (Portuguese)

The "Fátima Pope" with his godson, Duke Duarte of Bragança (far right)

Duke Duarte continued his primary education in Oporto (which he had started in Bern), and his secondary education first in the Nuno Álvares in Santo Tirso, and later at the Military College in Lisbon. Then he attended the superior course of Agronomic Engineering at the Agronomic Institute of the Technical University of Lisbon and the Institute for Development of the University of Geneva, Switzerland.

Since the accession to the Throne of St. Peter of Pope John Paul II, he and the Duke of Bragança had several private meetings at the Vatican.[83]

The Lost Monarchy of Portugal

It is interesting to add, that Our Lady's first apparition in Fátima took place soon after the last Portuguese king, Carlos I, was assassinated by the anti-clericals' revolution in 1910, and the last of the heirs, king Manuel II was forced into exile where he died in 1932. The kingdom was replaced with an imposed republic.

As mentioned above, Duke Duarte was born in exile. Interestingly, while in exile, the heir to the throne of Portugal also became the godson of Pope Pius XII, the first Pope to attempt the consecration to the Immaculate Heart. On February 15, 2005, Duke Duarte officially attended Sister Lucia's funeral at her convent at Coimbra and paid his respects.

---

83 Official Site of the Duke of Bragança, http://www.duque-de-braganca.com/page005. htm (Portuguese)

Our Holy Father after a meeting with Duke Duarte of Bragança, rightful heir to the royal throne of Portugal.

Our Lady's apparitions in Portugal can be viewed as those of a Queen who comes to claim her rights over a nation after her last representative has been eliminated. What is even more striking is the fact that to this date, there has never been any official document or act attempting to revoke King João IV's official royal proclamation of Our Lady's Queenship over Portugal. Our Fátima friend was right to exclaim with pride, "In Portugal the dogma of faith will always be preserved because Our Lady is the Queen of Portugal."

The Historical Heavenly Protection of Portugal

It is not my intention to imply either that all of the Portuguese people have responded to the message of Fátima or that the nation of Portugal has not been without its trials. Unfortunately, where God is at work so is his diabolical enemy. Secret evil societies have been at work, controlling governments and means of communication since the nation's beginning. These societies have attempted to bring down the moral fabric of the Portuguese nation through a heavy infiltration of pornography through the media, but somehow the Portuguese faithful have always taken recourse to their Queen at the right times. Many Portuguese families have begun to fight back.

On May 13, 1931, all the Bishops of Portugal, assisted by the Papal

Nuncio, gathered in Fátima and consecrated their country to the Immaculate Heart of Mary. At least 300,000 Portuguese pilgrims witnessed the event. Sister Lucia wrote and told her confessor that she understood that World War II was about to break out. She also told him that God had informed her that there would be a special protection of Portugal by the Immaculate Heart of Mary. This would happen to be due to the act of consecration made by the bishops in union with the faithful. Amazingly, as we have discussed before, while most of Europe suffered the scourge of the war, Portugal was providentially spared of its horrors. The Mother protected her children.

In 1974-1975, the communists attempted to take over Portugal. They temporarily got control of the government of Portugal, seizing all newspapers and mediums of communication. The Portuguese people responded by beginning a crusade of rosaries in reparation to the Immaculate Heart of their Heavenly Mother. Miraculously, the Communists began to lose domination over the country. Shortly after, the bishops of the country came to Fátima and renewed the consecration of the country on May 13th of 1975. Over a million pilgrims were present. The Communists were defeated!

9

The Apocalyptic Role of Pope John Paul II's Legacy

Interestingly, seven-year-old Jacinta, the youngest of the visionaries would often claim that she had been granted special visions of a Pope whom she called "the Holy Father." One day, after a vision, she even told her cousin Lucia: "Didn't you see the Holy Father? ...I don't know how it was, but I saw the Holy Father in a very big house,

kneeling by a table, with his head in his hands, and he was weeping. Outside the house, there were many people. Some of them were throwing stones. Others were cursing him and using bad language. Poor Holy Father, we must pray very much for him." Some time later while praying with her cousins at the cave she asked them, "Can't you see all those highways and roads and fields full of people, who are crying with hunger and have nothing to eat and the Holy Father in a church praying before the Immaculate Heart of Mary? And so many people praying with him?"[84]

Obviously the littlest visionary was granted visions of a Pope, a Pope who would endure much suffering. Who was this Pope? No identity was ever given to the children, and none of the three humble shepherds had even seen their current pope at the time. So, who was the Pope of the secret?

As we mentioned before, while recuperating in the Gemelli Clinic

84 *In Sister Lucia's Own Words*. (Memoirs of Sister Lucia) Volume 1. Secretariado Dos Pastorinhos, Fátima, Portugal.

in Rome Pope John Paul II asked for the envelope containing the third part of the secret. He received it on July 18, 1981, and returned it to the archives of the Holy Office on August 11, 1981. Upon leaving the clinic he shared: "I have come to understand that the only way to save the world from war, to save it from atheism, is the conversion of Russia according to the message of Fátima."

Pope John Paul II immediately felt the calling to consecrate the world to the Immaculate Heart of Mary and he himself composed a prayer for what he called an "Act of Entrustment." This means that reading the "third part" motivated Pope John Paul II to work hard for the Collegial Consecration. Why? Why him? What did he realize through the reading of the secret? Was he the Pope that little Jacinta was praying for? Sister Lucia confirmed his identity.

A year later, on May 13, 1982, Pope John Paul II visited Fátima to thank Our Lady for saving his life during the assassination attempt and while in Fátima, he made an act of Consecration to the Immaculate Heart. Sister Lucia came to Fátima to be present at the Mass with the Pope. She later told him that this 1982 consecration attempt was not done according to Our Lady's requests, for it needed the collegial participation of all the bishops.

This Marian Pope was not about to give up in honoring the request of the Lady from Heaven and searched for another date for the event. Finally, the long awaited moment arrived: March 25, 1984, the Feast of the Annunciation! This was the same date chosen 338 years previously by King João IV! Did this simple Portuguese king ever dream of the role he was playing? The Pope was about to do for the world, what King João had done for Portugal. Both acted on the belief that divine intervention had protected them from an attempt on their lives! They both understood well the authority entrusted to them.

The Pope made a touching and unprecedented move in history. He requested that the precious Portuguese image of Our Lady from the Shrine of Fátima be flown to the Vatican for the ceremony. The Portuguese church authorities agreed and Our Lady's image came to the See of Peter. On the morning of the Feast of the Annunciation, the long awaited moment finally came. Before a crowd of thousands and countless television cameras, the Holy Father changed the course of history by officially consecrating the world to the Immaculate Heart of Mary. These are his words:

1984 Consecration of the world before the image of Our Lady of Fátima

Behold, as we stand before you, Mother of Christ, before your Immaculate Heart, we desire, together with the whole Church, to unite ourselves with the consecration which, for love of us, Your Son made of Himself to the Father... We wish to unite ourselves with our Redeemer in this His consecration of the world and for the human race. ... The Power of consecration lasts for all time and embraces all individuals, peoples and nations... In entrusting to you, O Mother, the world, all individuals and peoples, we also entrust to you this very consecration of the world, placing it in your motherly heart.

The consecration of the world had taken place. The Vicar of Christ, in virtue of his jurisdiction had consecrated to the *Woman* what Adam had surrendered to the serpent. Was this enough? Would God accept it? Had all the bishops participated? For the 1984 Consecration, Pope John Paul II, in obedience to Our Lady's wishes, had written to all Catholic bishops of the world. Unfortunately it is suspected that not every Catholic bishop actually joined in the consecration. After the Pope's ceremony, when sister Lucia was told this, she responded: "It is true that not every Catholic bishop responded to the pope's request. That is their personal responsibility. Because of these bishops, God did not refuse to accept the Act of Consecration of 1984 as the act of union, which met the necessary conditions. But it was done right in 1984, and Our Lord has accepted the collegial consecration. The Lord will keep his word."[85]

On October 13, 1991, the author of the present work was personally blessed with the mission, given by the organizers of an American Marian ministry, of being the carrier of a letter to Sister Lucia. After the celebration of Mass at the convent's chapel in Coimbra, the letter for Sister Lucia was given to the Carmelite sisters by our pilgrimage's spiritual director. The very next spring in 1992, the author was blessed again, when the organizers called him to translate from the Portuguese language, Sister Lucia's response to the letter he had delivered. It was a humble little card with a short message typed on it. It read: "Dear... Regarding your question 'if the consecration made by John Paul II was accomplished according to Our Lady's requests...' Yes it was accomplished." She added "I receive all my letters and answer them personally." How could one have any further doubts? This author had personally delivered the letter to the convent in Coimbra, and witnessed the sisters' reception of it on behalf of Sister Lucia. Later he had received and translated her response. There could be no doubt!

The 1984 Consecration and "Absence of the Mention of Russia"

Nevertheless, some dissidents attempt to create doubt regarding the 1984 Consecration, claiming that Pope John Paul II failed to mention the name of Russia specifically. While pretending to be concerned with the conversion of Russia, they cleverly attack the image of the Holy Father, accusing him of disobedience to Our Lady's requests, and claiming that Sr. Lucia was being oppressed and forced into silence. What is the truth? Was the Pope disobedient? Why did he avoid the mention of Russia?

In order to understand this fully, we must first take another look at Pope Pius XII, as he was unjustly accused by the anti-Catholic media of not directly accusing and publicly condemning Hitler at the time that he had millions of Catholics under his authority even in Germany. This wise Pope knew that although he himself could launch a "condemnation" from the safety of the Vatican, he could not prevent the retaliations from Hitler against

---

85   Fr. Robert Fox, *Fátima Today: The Third Millennium*. Park Press Quality Printing. 2001. pp. 262-263.

millions of Catholics in the invaded nations. Moreover countless witnesses testify that Pius XII's wisdom and discretion saved millions of Jews. Jewish scientist Albert Einstein declared: "Only the Church stood squarely across the path of Hitler's campaign for sup-

Our Pope John Paul II and Sister Lucia

pressing truth. I had never any special interest in the Church before, but now I feel a great admiration because the Church alone has had the courage and persistence to stand for intellectual truth and moral freedom." [86]

The Chief Rabbi of Rome, Israel Zolli was so impressed by the altruistic work of Pope Pius XII during World War II, that in 1944 he entered the Catholic faith. As his baptismal name, he took the same one that the Pope had, Eugenio, as his own. Later he wrote a book entitled, *Why I Became a Catholic.*[87] Pinchas E. Lapide, Israeli Consul in Italy wrote: "The Catholic Church under Pius XII was instrumental in saving 860,000 Jews from Nazi death camps."

Pope Pius XII saved the lives of many Jews without imprudently risking the lives of numerous Catholic nuns, priests and faithful in the Nazi dominated nations. Thus Catholics need not be ashamed or apologetic, but rather proud of the Pope's stature as a moral leader.

Regarding the "absence of the mention of Russia" by Pope John Paul II during the 1984 consecration, again, there is no "cloak and dagger" behind it. Rather, much like the decision made by his predecessor, Pius XII, we find ourselves in the presence of another tactful, responsible and

---

86 Albert Einstein, *Time* magazine, December 23, 1940 issue. p. 38.
87 Pope Pius XII and the Holocaust, users.binary.net/polycarp/piusxii.html

wise judgment made by the Vicar of Christ. The Pope made a veiled but transparent allusion to Russia with the plea, "Enlighten especially the people whose consecration and entrusting you are awaiting from us." Nevertheless, many, who claim to be more Catholic than the Pope, became caught up in the fact that John Paul II, did not publicly mention the name Russia. in his words of consecration. Why?

These "critics" forget that in March of 1984, the Communist Iron Curtain had not collapsed yet! Millions of Catholics in Poland, Ukraine, and all the rest of the suppressed nations were still under the threat of the Communist leaders who since John Paul II's papal election had constantly kept a watchful eye on every move he made. The Pope was not only concerned about his personal safety inside the diplomatic immunity of the Vatican, but also for all the children entrusted to him by the Master. Could these Communist leaders perceive the mention of Russia as an embarrassing accusation and retaliate against the Church in Poland and in other Soviet oppressed nations? John Paul II chose wisdom, but what he bound was bound in Heaven. In his last book, the pope humbly recognized: "I know it is not I alone who acts in what I do as the Successor of Peter."[88]

According to Sister Lucia, Heaven accepted this consecration. She affirmed, "Now God will keep his word", and she was obviously right! Many changes, including the fall of the Berlin Wall, soon came to pass in East Germany and the Soviet Union without a bullet being fired. The world recognized the amazing historical role of John Paul II. This was acknowledged by world leaders and confirmed by the words of former U.S. President Bill Clinton to the pope, "We honor you for helping to lead a revolution of values and spirit in Central Europe and the former Soviet Union; freeing millions to live by conscience, not coercion; and freeing all of us from the constant fear of nuclear war." [89]

On May 13th, 2007, the main celebrant at the 90th Fátima anniversary, the Archbishop of Moscow Tadeusz Kondrusiewicz expressed: *We, in Russia, feel a special connection with the message of Fátima. In fact, the words that Our Lady pronounced on the day of July 13, 1917 do emphasize the extraordinary role, I will say, mysterious, of our country.... One thing however is certain: in the context of the modern nations, Russia is in a special way, under the direct protection of the Mother of God, which permits*

---

88 John Paul II, *Memory And Identity*. Rizzoli International Publications, New York. p. 165.
89 President William Clinton, January 26, 1999 – *The Life & Legacy of John Paul II* Coincide Publishing, LLC. 2005, p. 48.

the nourishing of hope. Therefore, it would be a great sin if we forgot the message of Fátima, "the most prophetic of the modern apparitions." [90]

When speaking of the reason for the large pilgrimage of Russians for the 90th October anniversary at Fátima, the Archbishop of Moscow added: *Our private intention is to thank our Mother, the Most Holy Virgin, for the gift of religious liberty. We have also the intention to pray for the gift of the authentic conversion and the rebirth of the Russian society.... The pilgrimage of the image of Our Lady of Fátima across the vast territory of Russia and of Kazakhstan in the year of 1996 became in itself "the national spiritual exercise". Our churches were flooded with people, they came to pray before the Pilgrim Mother of God, not only the Catholics but also the Orthodox. Only God knows how many persons went to confession and received communion, and how many conversions were the fruit of the pilgrimage. May God be always praised by what He does through the intercession of Our Lady of Fátima.*[91]

Sister Lucia's Last Message for the World: *No more secrets!*

On November 17, 2001 it was considered necessary by the Vatican for Archbishop Tarsciso Bertone to go personally to meet with Sister Lucia

Sr. Maria Lucia of Jesus and the Immaculate Heart

to clarify and to obtain information from her. This was necessary because of the onset of rumors of suspicion that the Holy See had not published the entire text of the third secret. The meeting lasted more than two hours. Sister Lucia replied, *Everything has been published; there are no more secrets. If I had received new revelations, I would not have communicated them to anyone, but I would have told them directly to the Holy Father.*[92]

Sister Maria Celina, the Con-

---

90 Interview realized by *LeopolDina Reis Simões*-Sala de Imprensa of the Social Communications Center of the Fátima Shrine. Bulletin May 19, 2007
91 Ibid.
92 http://www.ewtn.com/vnews/getstory.sap?number=53877

vent's superior said that Sister Lucia always denied any talk of a *fourth secret of Fatima*. She declared that Sister Lucia would say of people who spread rumors of the alleged secret that *they are never satisfied; that they should do what Our Lady asked, that this is the most important thing. When someone would say: "Sister Lucia, they say there is another secret"[...] she would look at them ironically. "If there is one," she would say, "I wish they would tell it to me: I know of no other secrets."* [93]

Let us not be deceived by dissenting people who argue that Russia is not yet converted. Let us remember that our free Western world is not converted yet either, regardless of all the blessings it has received. God has not forced His will on the West; He will not force it on the Russian people. Let's not forget that it took nearly eighty years of atrocities and abuse to destroy the faith of many in those nations. Healing those memories will not happen overnight, but God is working!

If any so-called "Marian" publication attempts to place doubt on the holiness and spirituality of the late Sister Lucia or our recently deceased Vicar of Christ, let us remember that this so-called "oppressed nun" was the same brave little child who in 1917, did not cower under the threats of "being boiled in oil," to betray the testimony that she had been given from Heaven. This holy Pope, accused of being "afraid to mention Russia", was dangerously wounded and still remained tireless traveling around the world, under threats to his life, taking the Gospel to all the corners of the world.

John Paul II was constantly reminding us that the important and often disregarded message of Fátima is still very crucial. This is the reason that he went to Fátima on May 13, 2000. He aimed to open our eyes to the overlooked *apocalyptic* meaning of Fátima. By means of the beatification at the beginning of the century, he brought Fátima into the Third Millennium. By this move, he invited the world to *take a second look* at what the Lady from Heaven came down to reveal in 1917. Why?

---

93 "Sister Lucia's Last Moments". Zenit News Agency September 25th, 2007

John Paul II's Legacy and the Unknown Dimension of Fátima

In reference to the young visionaries, John Paul II remarked, "Jesus and his Mother often choose children and give them important tasks for the life of the Church and of humanity."[94] He obviously believed that the Message of Fátima was of immense importance for the future life of humanity.

We have explored the different dimensions of Fátima, e.g. the catechetical dimension of a Mother instructing her children about the truths and mysteries concerning their future home. We have also explored the Biblical dimension, which amazingly reveals to us the connection of the Fátima message with the events that took place in the Garden of Eden, calling us to the consecration of a world once surrendered by Adam to the Evil One. We have also traveled through the historical dimension of Fátima, discovering Heaven's intervention during humanity's most painful

---

94   John Paul II, *Christmas Letter to the World's Children*. Origins. January 5, 1995. p. 485.

trials. Finally, we discovered the apocalyptic dimension of Fátima, which involved the person of one amazing man, John Paul II.

It is not difficult to believe that Our Lady's request for the consecration of the world was already in the Creator's mind at the time of the fall. Such task would be demanding, the spiritual battle would be unspeakable. It would take a very special spiritual and obedient human person to accomplish it, a person like John Paul II.

As we have read, several popes opened and read the third secret without feeling personally called to act upon it. They probably sensed that it did not apply to them. It was meant for the man whose life was saved by the "hand of Our Lady". In his testament, he recalled the 1981 attempt on his life and said that the "Lord of life and death himself prolonged my life, in a certain way, he gave it to me again. From that moment, it belonged to him even more."[95]

This pope was "the Marian Pope of all times." His devotion to the Mother of God was inspiring. From the moment of his papal election, he guided the Church towards the important role of the only mother he ever had, the Blessed Virgin Mary. He entrusted his pontificate to her protection through his papal motto *Totus Tuus*, (totally yours) which originated from his own Marian consecration.

Pope John Paul II has been taken from us, but not before leaving us a priceless and immeasurable legacy. He was a Pope with a Mother! He had an incomparable Marian devotion and a profound communion with the Mother of Our Lord, and his actions and his words reflected it. He was the most powerful spiritual leader on earth yet he felt that he was personally guided by her maternal hand. He taught us to rediscover and to accept the Mother of Jesus as our own personal mother. He taught our world how to trust in her and in her loving intercession with her Divine Son. Pope Benedict XVI recently commented, "With his words and even more so with his example, Pope John Paul II taught us to contemplate Christ with Mary's eyes, valuing especially the prayer of the holy rosary,"[96]

John Paul II directed our gaze to our Heavenly Mother through his untiring pilgrimage journeys to almost all the Marian Shrines of the world. From Czestochowa, Poland to Guadalupe in Mexico; and from Lourdes, France to Loretto, Italy; this pope constantly guided our hearts to the loving

---

95 *Papal Testament: Fate Was in God's Hands*, Zenit News Organization. Vatican City, April 8, 2005
96 Pope Benedict XVI, *Regina Caeli Message*. Vatican City. Sunday May 1, 2005 - Zenit News Agency.

message of Mary. There is one Marian shrine, however, that became of tremendous and crucial importance during his papacy. This was Fátima. It could almost appear that John Paul II formed part of mystery of Fátima since he was born. Providence placed him on earth 90 days after little Jacinta's death and he was taken 48 days after Sr. Lucia's passing. The Fátima apparitions of 1917 and the life of Karol Wojtyla, which began in 1920, were two historical events which God's Providence predestined for an encounter. These two trajectories came to a fated collision at St. Peter's Square on May 13, 1981 at the assassination attempt. From this point on, the Pope's mission would never be the same. The Lady's Fátima message became part of his papacy. Later, Pope Benedict XVI, aware of this special bond, would choose the day May 13, 2005 to announce the official dispensation for the established five-year waiting period, to open his cause of beatification.[97]

Pope John Paul II realized that the message given to three Portuguese children in 1917 was, and would continue to be, of enormous importance for humanity. It contains a solemn and stern request from God that could change the world forever! At Fátima, the Creator, through Our Lady's intercession, called for the consecration of Russia to the Immaculate Heart of Mary. A message so severe and vital, that it took an assassin's bullet to stress its importance. It led this holy pope to the very special land of Portugal

Like John Paul II, Portugal seems to have been nurtured and prepared by the hand of Our Lady herself. Yes, Portugal has been prepared for its mission. It has been prepared through the actions of its faithful kings. It has been prepared

In Portugal, the dogma of faith will always be preserved

97 *"Waiting Period Waived for John Paul II."* Zenit News Agency, May 13, 2005

through the faithful Marian devotion and suffering of its people. Finally, it has been prepared through the heavenly intervention of its Heavenly Mother and Queen.

When John Paul II entrusted the world to the Immaculate Heart of Mary on March 25, 1984, he was doing for the world, what King João IV had done for Portugal on March 25, 1646. He was placing that which had been "entrusted to him" into the caring hands of the Queen of Heaven. He could not do this by himself. For this entrustment or consecration to be valid in the eyes of God, it also needed the participation of the people of God and the Church. The Portuguese people lined up behind their king in support of his proclamation. The Pope needed us and the College of Bishops behind him in his consecration of the world to the Immaculate Heart.

The Lady's request became an essential part of his mission and he was not about to fail. He knew that our future depended on it. He set out to consecrate the world to her Immaculate Heart regardless of the personal cost. He obediently attempted the act more than once: first, on May 13, 1982; later, in collegiality with most of the bishops on March 25, 1984. Finally, he entrusted the whole world, in union with all the world bishops in attendance to Rome on October 8, 2000. Each time, he did it in front of the precious image of Our Lady from the Shrine of Fátima. He also consecrated personally every nation he visited. His apocalyptic mission had been accomplished!

Why Fátima? Because the final "battle of the creatures" is at hand. As the announced triumph of the Immaculate becomes imminent, the climactic showdown between the "ancient evil serpent" and the *Woman of the Apocalypse* becomes nearer. We, the children of the world, are being

**Portuguese pilgrims entering
their Mother's shrine of Fátima**

called to choose whose side we desire to be on. A large majority of the Portuguese have already made that choice.

On November 12th of 2004, Pope John Paul II welcomed the visit of Portugal's president Jorge Sampaio and praised him for his nation's faithful Catholicism, saying, **"The world continues to look to Portugal with hope, especially in terms of becoming aware of the grave crisis of values in modern society, ever more insecure in the face of fundamental ethical decisions for the future path of humanity."**

At the beginning of his last visit with the Portuguese president, the Pope recalled his visit to Fátima of 2000, to beatify "...the two great Portuguese little ones: Francisco and Jacinta Marto." He exclaimed: **"The special light that shone in their lives wants to illuminate the world. The world continues to look to Portugal with hope."**[98]

Yes, the message of Fátima reminds us of the tremendous importance of praying the Rosary. It also stresses the precious heavenly protection that comes from wearing the brown scapular. They are both tremendous gifts from heaven and we should appreciate them and we make grateful use of them. But, the Lady of Fátima came to Portugal to help the world discover much more.

On May 13, 2006, Cardinal Stanislaw Dziwisz, Archbishop of Krakow and John Paul II's personal secretary and confidant was the main celebrant at the Anniversary Mass in Fátima. He was in the jeep during the attempt on the Pope's life. His homily was very revealing of his intimate understanding of John Paul II's special mission: *We believe that, by God's design, Mary's protection is not merely limited to our spiritual life, but it includes all to our daily existence.... Guided by this conviction, we are able to say that twenty-five years ago a miracle took place, precisely thanks to the protection of Mary. Thanks to Her intercession, Pope John Paul II was saved, being gravelly injured by the deadly bullet of the assassin. John Paul II himself believed firmly that "one hand had fired, but another one had guided the bullet."*

Expressing tremendous admiration, he continued: Today - I am certain! - John Paul II is now in the Father's House, but we do not forget what he had to experience. We continue to thank Our Lord and his Most Holy Mother for his life, which was consumed for twenty-four consecutive long years in the faithful service of God, of the Church and of the entire humanity. It was for this reason that I received with good will the invitation

---

98 *"Pope Encourages Portugal to Form a Critical Conscience"* Zenit, Vatican City, Nov. 12, 2004 www.zenit.org

made by the Bishop of Fátima for me to come here to preside at this solemn liturgy. I am a humble servant of this great Pope and, at the same time, a fortunate witness of his holiness. For this reason I came here: to give thanks, to express my personal gratitude and the gratitude of the Church of Krakow, now entrusted to my pastoral care by Pope Benedict XVI. It is a gratitude expressed in unison for the extraordinary gift of God manifested in the pontificate of John Paul II.

A pontificate initiated - who does not remember it? - with that courageous appeal made to all the men and women of the world: "Do not be afraid. Open, instead open wide the doors to Christ!". A pontificate lived each day with the daily repetition of the motto: "Totus tuus, Maria", and not only with words, but very real with a spirit of total dedication even up to the last days of his agony and at the very moment of his death. Without a doubt, thanks to such dedication, the fulfillment of the message that Mary had given to the little Shepherds took place in our days. In fact, after the attack of May 13, 1981, he himself asked for the envelope that contained the third part of the secret.

As it is known, he immediately thought of the consecration of the world to the Immaculate Heart of Mary, having himself composed a prayer for the so called "Act of Entrustment" that was going to be celebrated in the Basilica of Saint Maria Major in the solemnity of the Day of Pentecost, on the day of June 7, 1981. Seeing himself forcefully prevented from being present, the Pope delivered it through his locution in a radio message. These were his words: "Ó Mother of peoples and all nations, receive our outcry, guided in the Holy Spirit directly to your heart, and embrace it with the love of the Mother and of the Lord's Servant, all those that await for this embrace and at the same time all those whose entrustment You expect in a particular manner. Take under Your maternal protection the entire human family that, with affectionate delight, we entrust to You, ó Mother. May it bring about for all, the arrival of the times of peace and of liberty, the times of truth, of justice and of hope."

In order to respond more fully to the requests of "Our Lady", our Holy Father wanted to set out, during the Holy Year of the Redemption, that Act of Entrustment of the 7th of June of 1981 and that he had repeated here, in Fátima, on May 13 of 1982. And so, on the day that is remembered by the fiat pronounced by Mary in the moment of the Annunciation, on March 25, 1984 in the Plaza of Saint Peter, the Pope, in spiritual union with all of the previously "summoned" Bishops of the world, entrusted *the people and the nations to the Immaculate Heart of Mary. Sister Lucia personally confirmed that such solemn and universal act of consecration corresponded with that which Our Lady desired.*

This act could not fail, when the truth of Mary's words had already been experienced: "If my requests are heeded, Russia will be converted, and there will be peace, if not she will spread her errors throughout the world, etc." There had been too much blood, too many horrors had spread throughout the world, because the requests of Our Lady still they had not been heeded. And, to the contrary, how many things have changed in Europe and in the world since 1981 up to today. The atheistic Communism was defeated, and today the oppressed nations can live in peace. We cannot fail to thank Our Lord for the fulfillment of Mary's promise. And we are also grateful to John Paul II for his wisdom, docility and courage.[99]

Our Holy Father John Paul II understood the mystery of the message of Fátima. He bequeathed that precious knowledge to us in the following words: **"Mary's message at Fátima can be summed up in the words with which Christ began his preaching, 'the kingdom of God is at hand, repent and believe in the Gospel.' As the Third Millennium draws near, that message remains timely, especially in the light of the events of the last decades: The providential changes which have recently taken place in the countries of Central and Eastern Europe."**[100]

John Paul II has left the world, but he did not leave us orphans, he left us a world entrusted to the Immaculate Heart of Mary for the Third Millennium. That was his apocalyptic mission! This was his legacy! Now it is up to us which side of the battle we choose. He left us with this final fatherly warning: **"The message of Fátima is a call to conversion, alerting humanity to have nothing to do with the 'dragon' whose 'tail swept down a third of the stars of heaven, and cast them to the earth'"**[101]

Those who have ears to hear... listen!

99   Fátima Anniversary Homily. May 13th, 2006, Cardinal *Stanislaw Dziwisz*, Archbishop of Krakow
100   John Paul II, Papal Audience at Vatican City. May 15, 1991.
101   John Paul II, Beatification Homily, Fátima, May 13, 2000.

Epilogue

But in Portugal,
the Dogma of Faith will Always be Preserved

I have been blessed with the opportunity of visiting many wonderful Marian Shrines during my life. At all of them I have experienced the grace of God and the loving presence of His Mother. One can sense the Mother's call for her children's return to Her Son. Nine pilgrimages I have made to Fátima. What I found striking about Fátima is that, there, you witness not only the Mother's call, but also the children's response.

The Day of the Children,
20,000 Portuguese children attended

In the past, some of the Portuguese Catholic faithful embraced the call to the Rosary so seriously that they began to measure distances, not by minutes of walking, but by the decades of the Rosary that they prayed while getting there. It was not surprising to hear older natives of the region of Fátima giving directions such as *"It is about a Rosary and a decade from here."*

But, the Portuguese faithful are also investing in their future. Every year on June 10th, they celebrate solemnly the Feast of the Guardian Angel of Portugal. Around this day they celebrate "O Dia das Crianças" (Day of the Children). Hundreds of thousands of children arrive in caravans of buses at the Fátima shrine for the celebration. Their families also attend. The focus of the religious activities is to help the children realize the True Presence of Jesus in the Eucharist. The children are invited to meditate on the words and actions of the angel who prostrated himself before the Host while repeating; "My God, I believe, I adore, I hope and I love You; and I beg pardon for all those who do not believe, do not adore, do not hope and do not love You." How can this nation not receive blessings in the future? What can we learn from them?

During the Beatification John Paul II spoke to the Portuguese children, many of them dressed like the little shepherds: "My last words are for the children: dear boys and girls, I see so many of you dressed like Francisco and Jacinta. You look very nice! But in a little while or tomorrow you will take these clothes off and ... the little shepherds will disappear. They should not disappear, should they?! Our Lady needs

you all to console Jesus, who is sad because of the bad things done to him; He needs your prayers and your sacrifices for sinners."

Portuguese children dressed as the 3 shepherds

John Paul II had a great devotion to the message of Fátima. His whole life was changed by the events that took place there. He believed that the destiny of human history had been altered by the testimony of a nine-year old child and her two younger cousins! He also believed in spiritual capacity of children. In his 1994 Christmas Letter to the children, he wrote:

"Just as Jesus in the Gospel shows special trust in children, so His mother Mary in the course of history has not failed to show her motherly care to the little ones. Think of Saint Bernadette of Lourdes, the children of La Salette and in our own century Lucia, Francisco and Jacinta of Fátima.... Jesus and his Mother often choose children and give them important tasks for the life of the Church and of humanity. I have named only a few who are known everywhere, but how many others there are who are less widely known!" [102]

Later, at the Vatican John Paul II said, "For my part, I accompany you with prayer so that, like Jesus, you may grow in wisdom and grace, before God and men. This will happen if you always love Our Lady and let her guide you. May the example of the shepherd children of Fátima, Francesco and Jacinta, whom this very year I had the joy of beatifying, show once again that children have a special bond with the Virgin Mary. With her help, they can reach the peaks of holiness." [103]

In conclusion, when I invested time in the study of Fátima, I discovered that it was not just another short visit from the Heavenly Mother to her children. It was not only about praying the Rosary and wearing the brown scapular; it was far more than that. Fátima is probably the greatest Marian apparition of the 20th

Portuguese Shrine of Our Lady of Fátima, Portugal

century and its apocalyptic consequences may be eternal. Although it happened over nine decades ago and all three of the young visionaries are already enjoying their eternal rest, Fátima is not over! The Message of Fátima was of tremendous importance to two wonderful people. It was of tremendous concern to a Pope that was busy promoting its message until his last breath. It also concerned a sweet little shepherd girl who eighty-seven years earlier, was left on the earth a bit longer so that she could promote devotion to the Immaculate Heart of the Heavenly Lady.

Fátima is unfolding and it contains biblical and apocalyptic repercussions for all humanity, even in the Third Millennium. Sadly,

102 John Paul II, *Christmas Letter to the World's Children* Origins. January 5, 1995 p. 485.
103 H. H. John Paul II's address to the young people of Italian Catholic Action, Thursday 21, December 2000.

nearly 90 years have passed, and a majority of the faithful still ignore or overlook the true importance of Fátima. During a rare interview in 1992, Sister Lucia was asked if she had a message for the world. "Just one" she answered, "those who desire to be one the side of God must be with the Pope. Those who are not with the Pope are not on the side of God."[104]

Was Sister Lucia correct? Even non-religious news media and many world leaders have credited John Paul II with effecting the change of the Soviet Union and consequently the whole world. I believe that the Heavenly Message of Fátima is like a volcano that began to boil in 1917, and is now about to erupt! Most of the "protagonists" in this mission, Jacinta, Francisco, Lucia, the 70,000 eyewitnesses, and Pope John Paul II have already gone to Heaven to their Eternal reward. Those few remaining will probably be called soon. The world was given an amazing heavenly gift. Did we take the trouble to unwrap it, open and appreciate it? The future of humanity is still at stake and the message of Fátima has much to say about it. *We are now in the Third Millennium, are we finally going to listen?*

---

104 Carlos Evaristo, *Two Hours with Sister Lucy.* 1992.

Appendix I

Pope John Paul's First Pilgrimage to Portugal

MASS IN THE SHRINE OF OUR LADY OF THE ROSARY

HOMILY OF POPE JOHN PAUL II
Fatima May 13, 1982

On Thursday, May 13th, the second day of Pope John Paul's pilgrimage to Portugal, the Holy Father visited Fatima to commemorate in a very special way the first anniversary of the attempt on his life and the sixty-fifth anniversary of Our Lady's first apparition at Fatima.

"And from that hour ..."

1. "And from that hour the disciple took her to his own home" (Jn 19:27).

   These are the concluding words of the Gospel in today's liturgy at Fatima. The disciple's name was John. It was he, John, the son of Zebedee, the apostle and evangelist, who heard from the Cross the words of Christ: "Behold, your mother". But first Christ had said to his Mother: "Woman, behold, your son". This was a wonderful testament.

   As he left this world, Christ gave to his Mother a man, a human being, to be like a son for her: John. He entrusted him to her. And, as a consequence of this giving and entrusting, Mary became the mother of John. The Mother of God became the Mother of man.

   From that hour John "took her to his own home" and became the earthly guardian of the Mother of his Master; for sons have the right and duty to care for their mother. John became by Christ's will the son of the Mother of God. And in John every human being became her child.

The Mother's presence

2. The words "he took her to his own home" can be taken in the literal sense as referring to the place where he lived.

Mary's motherhood in our regard is manifested in a particular way in the places where she meets us: her dwelling places; places in which a special presence of the Mother is felt.

There are many such dwelling places. They are of all kinds: from a special corner in the home or little wayside shrines adorned with an image of the Mother of God, to chapels and churches built in her honor. However, in certain places; the Mother's presence is felt in a particularly vivid way. These places sometimes radiate their light over a great distance and draw people from afar. Their radiance may ex tend over a diocese, a whole nation, or at times over several countries and even continents. These places are the Marian sanctuaries or shrines.

In all these places that unique testament of the Crucified Lord is wonderfully actualized: in them man feels that he is entrusted and confided to Mary; he goes there in order to be with her as with his Mother he opens his heart to her and speaks to her about everything: he "takes her to his own home", that is to say, he brings her into all his problems, which at times are difficult, ... His own problems ...and those of others. The problems of the family, of societies, of nations' and of the whole of humanity.

Through God's mercy

3. Is not this the case with the shrine at Lourdes, in France? Is not this the case with Jasna Gora, in Poland, my own country's shrine, which this year is celebrating its six hundredth anniversary?

    There too, as in so many other shrines of Mary throughout the world, the words of today's liturgy seem to resound with a particularly authentic force: "You are the great pride of our nation" (Jdt 15:9), and also: "...when our nation was 'brought low'... you avenged our ruin, walking in the straight path before our God" (Jdt 13:20).

    At Fatima these words resound; as one particular echo of the experiences not only of the Portuguese nation but also of so many other countries and peoples on this earth: indeed, they echo the experience of modern mankind as a whole, the whole of the human family.

4. And so I come here today because on this very day last year, in Saint Peter's Square in Rome, the attempt on the Pope's life was made, in mysterious coincidence with the anniversary of the first apparition at Fatima, which occurred on 13 May 1917.

I seemed to recognize in the coincidence of the dates a special call to come to this place. And so, today I am here. I have come in order to thank Divine Providence in this place which the Mother of God seems to have chosen in a particular way. *Misericordiae Domini, quia non sumus consumpti* (Through God's mercy we were spared-Lam 3:22), I repeat once more with the prophet. I have come especially in order to confess here the glory of God himself: "Blessed be the Lord God, who created the heavens and the earth", I say in the words of today's liturgy (Jdt 13:18). And to the Creator of heaven and earth I also raise that special hymn of glory which is she herself, the Immaculate Mother of the Incarnate Word:

"O daughter, you are blessed by the Most High God above all women on earth... your hope will never de part from the hearts of men, as they remember the power of God. May; God grant this to be a perpetual honour to you" (Jdt 18:20).

The basis of this song of praise, which the Church lifts up with joy here as in so many other places on the earth, is the incomparable choice of a daughter of the human race to be the Mother of God.

And therefore let God above all be praised: Father, Son and Holy Spirit. May blessing and veneration be given to Mary, the model of the Church, as the "dwelling-place of the Most Holy Trinity".

Spiritual motherhood

5. From the time when Jesus, dying on the Cross, said to John: "Behold, your mother"; from the time when "the disciple took her to his own home", the mystery of the spiritual motherhood of Mary has been actualized boundlessly in history. Motherhood means caring for the life of the child. Since Mary is the mother of us all, her care for: the life of man is universal. The care of a mother embraces her child totally. Mary's motherhood has its beginning in her motherly care for Christ. In Christ, at the foot of the Cross, she accepted John, and in John she accepted all of us totally. Mary embraces us all with special solicitude in the Holy Spirit. For as we profess in our Creed, he is "the giver of life". It is he who gives the fullness of life, open towards eternity.

Mary's spiritual motherhood is therefore a sharing in the power of the Holy Spirit, of "the giver of life". It is the humble service of her who says of herself: "Behold, I am the handmaid of the Lord" (Lk 1:38).

In the light of the mystery of Mary's spiritual motherhood, let us seek to understand the extraordinary message, which began on 13 May, 1917 to resound throughout the world from Fatima, continuing for five months until 13 October of the same year.

Conversion and repentance

6. The Church has always taught and continues to proclaim that God's revelation was brought to completion in Jesus Christ, who is the fullness of that revelation, and that "no new public revelation is to be expected before the glorious manifestation of our Lord" (Dei Verbum, 4). The Church evaluates and judges private revelations by the criterion of conformity with that single public Revelation.

If the Church has accepted the message of Fatima, it is above all because that message contains a truth and a call whose basic content is the truth and the call of the Gospel itself. "Repent, and believe in the gospel" (Mk 1:15): these are the first words that the Messiah addressed to humanity. The message of Fatima is, in its basic nucleus, a call to conversion and repentance, as in the Gospel. This call was uttered at the beginning of the twentieth century, and it was thus addressed particularly to this present century. The Lady of the message seems to have read with special insight the "signs of the times", the signs of our time.

The call to repentance is a motherly one, and at the same time it is strong and decisive. The love that "rejoices in the truth" (cf. 1 Cor 13:) is capable of being clear-cut and firm. The call to repentance is linked, as always, with a call to prayer. In harmony with the tradition of many centuries, the Lady of the message indicates the Rosary, which can rightly be defined as "Mary's prayer": the prayer in which she feels particularly united with us. She herself prays with us. The rosary prayer embraces the problems of the Church, of the See of Saint Peter, the problems of the whole world. In it we also remember sinners, that they may be converted and saved, and the souls in Purgatory

The words of the message were addressed to children aged from seven to ten. Children, like Bernadette of Lourdes, are particularly privileged in these apparitions of the Mother of God. Hence the fact that also her language is simple, within the limits of their understanding. The children of Fatima became partners in dialogue with the Lady of the message and collaborators with her. One of them is still living.

Appendix I

A Mother's Love

7. When Jesus on the Cross said: "Woman, behold, your son" (Jn 19: 26), in a new way he opened his Mother's Heart, the Immaculate Heart, and revealed to it the new dimensions and extent of the love to which she was called in the Holy Spirit by the power of the sacrifice of the Cross.

In the words of Fatima we seem to find this dimension of motherly love, whose range covers the whole of man's path towards God; the path that leads through this world and that goes, through Purgatory, beyond this world. The solicitude of the Mother of the Saviour is solicitude for the work of salvation: the work of her Son. It is solicitude for the salvation, the eternal salvation, of all. Now that sixty-five years have passed since that 13 May 1917, it is difficult to fail to notice how the range of this salvific love of the Mother embraces, in a particular way, our century.

In the light of a mother's love we understand the whole message of the Lady of Fatima. The greatest obstacle to man's journey towards God is sin, perseverance in sin, and, finally, denial of God. The deliberate blotting out of God from the world of human thought. The detachment from him of the whole of man's earthly activity. The rejection of God by man.

In reality, the eternal salvation of man is only in God. Man's rejection of God, if it becomes definitive, leads logically to God's rejection of man (cf. Mt 7:23; 10:33), to damnation.

Can the Mother who with all the force of the love that she fosters in the Holy Spirit desires everyone's salvation keep silence on what undermines the very bases of their salvation? No, she cannot.

And so, while the message of Our Lady of Fatima is a motherly one, it is also strong and decisive. It sounds severe. It sounds like John the Baptist speaking on the banks of the Jordan. It invites to repentance. It gives a warning. It calls to prayer. It recommends the Rosary.

The message is addressed to every human being. The love of the Savior's Mother reaches every place touched by the work of salvation. Her care extends to every individual of our time, and to all the societies nations and peoples. Societies menaced by apostasy, threatened by moral degradation. The collapse of morality involves the collapse of societies.

Meaning of consecration

8. On the Cross Christ said: "Woman, behold, your son!" With these words he opened in a new way his Mother's heart. A little later, the Roman soldier's spear pierced the side of the Crucified One. That pierced heart became a sign of the redemption achieved through the death of the Lamb of God.

The Immaculate Heart of Mary, opened with the words "Woman, behold, your son!", is spiritually united with the heart of her Son opened by the soldier's spear. Mary's Heart was opened by the same love for man and for the world with which Christ loved man and the world, offering himself for them on the Cross, until the soldier's spear struck that blow.

Consecrating the world to the Immaculate Heart of Mary means drawing near, through the Mother's intercession, to the very Fountain of life that sprang from Golgotha. This Fountain pours forth unceasingly redemption and grace. In it reparation is made continually for the sins of the world. It is a ceaseless source of new life and holiness.

Consecrating the world to the Immaculate Heart of the Mother means returning beneath the Cross of the Son. It means consecrating this world to the pierced Heart of the Savior, bringing it back to the very source of its Redemption. Redemption is always greater than man's sin and the "sin of the world." The power of the Redemption is infinitely superior to the whole range of evil in man and the world.

The Heart of the Mother is aware of this, more than any other heart in the whole universe, visible and invisible.

And so she calls us. She not only calls us to be converted: she calls us to accept her motherly help to return to the source of Redemption.

Love for all persons

9. Consecrating ourselves to Mary means accepting her help to offer ourselves and the whole of mankind to Him who is Holy, infinitely Holy; it means accepting her help by having recourse to her motherly Heart, which beneath the Cross was opened to love for every human being, for the whole world in order to offer the: world, the individual human being, mankind as a whole, and all the nations to Him who is infinitely Holy. God's holiness showed itself in the redemption of man, of the world, of the whole of mankind, and of the nations: a redemption brought about through the Sacrifice of the Cross. *"For* *their sake I consecrate myself"*, Jesus had said (Jn 17:19).

By the power of the redemption the world and man have been consecrated. They have been consecrated to Him who is infinitely Holy. They have been offered and entrusted to Love itself, merciful Love.

The Mother of Christ calls us, invites us to join with the Church of the living God in the consecration of the world, in this act of confiding by which the world, mankind as a whole, the nations, and each individual person are presented to the Eternal Father with the power of the Redemption won by Christ. They are offered in the Heart of the Redeemer which was pierced on the Cross.

Rooted in the Gospel

10. The appeal of the Lady of the message of Fatima is so deeply rooted in the Gospel and the whole of Tradition that the Church feels that the message imposes a commitment on her.

She has responded through the Servant of God Pius XII (whose episcopal ordination took place precisely on 13 May 1917): he consecrated the human race and especially the Peoples of Russia to the Immaculate Heart of Mary. Was not that consecration his response to the evangelical eloquence of the call of Fatima?

In its Dogmatic Constitution on the Church (Lumen Gentium) and its Pastoral Constitution on the Church in the Modern World (Gaudium et Spes) the Second Vatican Council amply illustrated the reasons for the link between the Church and the world of today. Furthermore, its teaching on Mary's special place in the mystery of Christ and the Church bore mature fruit in Paul VI's action in calling Mary Mother of the Church and thus indicating more profoundly the nature of her union with the Church and of her care for the world, for mankind, for each human being, and for all the nations: what characterizes them is her motherhood. This brought a further deepening of understanding of the meaning of the act of consecrating that the Church is celled upon to perform with the help of the Heart of Christ's Mother and ours.

Many going astray

11. Today John Paul II, successor of Peter, continuer of the work of Pius, John, and Paul, and particular heir of the Second Vatican Council, presents himself before the Mother of the Son of God in her Shrine at

Fatima. In what way does he come?

He presents himself, reading again with trepidation the motherly call to penance, to conversion, the ardent appeal of the Heart of Mary that resounded at Fatima sixty-five years ago. Yes, he reads it again with trepidation in his heart, because he sees how many people and societies—how many Christians—have gone in the opposite direction to the one indicated in the message of Fatima. Sin has thus made itself firmly at home in the world, and denial of God has become widespread in the ideologies, ideas and plans of human beings.

But for this very reason the evangelical call to repentance and conversion, uttered in the Mother's message, remains ever relevant. It is still more relevant than it was sixty-five years ago. It is still more urgent. And so it is to be the subject of next year's Synod of Bishops, which we are already preparing for.

The successor of Peter presents himself here also as a witness to the immensity of human suffering, a witness to the almost apocalyptic menaces looking over the nations and mankind as a whole. He is trying to embrace these sufferings with his own weak human heart, as he places himself before the mystery of the Heart of the Mother, the Immaculate Heart of Mary.

In the name of these sufferings and with awareness of the evil that is spreading throughout the world and menacing the individual human being, the nations, and mankind as a whole, Peter's successor presents himself here with greater faith in the redemption of the world, in the saving Love that is always stronger, always more powerful than any evil.

My heart is oppressed when I see the sin of the world and the whole range of menaces gathering like a dark cloud over mankind, but it also rejoices with hope as I once more do what has been done by my Predecessors, when they consecrated the world to the Heart of the Mother, when they consecrated especially to that Heart those peoples which particularly need to be consecrated. Doing this means consecrating the world to Him who is infinite Holiness. This Holiness means redemption. It means a love more powerful than evil. No "sin of the world" can ever overcome this Love.

Once more this act is being done. Mary's appeal is not for just once. Her appeal must be taken up by generation after generation, in accordance with the ever new "signs of the times". It must be unceasingly returned to. It must ever be taken up anew.

Faith of the Church

12. The author of the Apocalypse wrote: "And I saw the holy city, new Jerusalem, coming down out of heaven from God, prepared as a bride adorned for her husband and I heard a loud voice from the throne saying, 'Behold, the dwelling of God is with men. He will dwell with them, and they shall be his people, and God himself will be with them'" (Rev 21:2-3).

This is the faith by which the Church lives. This is the faith with which the People of God makes its journey.

"The dwelling of God is with men" on earth even now. In that dwelling is the Heart of the Bride and Mother, Mary, a Heart adorned with the jewel of her Immaculate Conception. The heart of the Bride and Mother which was opened beneath the Cross by the word of her Son to a great new love for man and the world. The Heart of the Bride and Mother which is aware of all the sufferings of individuals and societies on earth.

The People of God is a pilgrim along the ways of this world in an eschatological direction. It is making its pilgrimage towards the eternal Jerusalem, towards "the dwelling of God with men." God will there "wipe away every tear from their eyes, and death shall be no more, neither shall there be mourning nor crying nor pain any more, for the former things have passed away"

But at present "the former things are still in existence. They it is that constitute the temporal setting of our pilgrimage.

For that reason we look towards "him who sits upon the throne and says, 'Behold, I make all things new'" (cf. Rev 21:5).

And together with the Evangelist and Apostle we try to see with the eyes of faith "the new heaven and the new earth"; for the first heaven and the first earth have passed away.

But "the first heaven and the first earth" still exist about us and within us. We cannot ignore it. But this enables us to recognize what an immense grace was granted to us human beings when, in the midst of our pilgrimage, there shone forth on the horizon of the faith of our times this "great portent, a woman" (cf. Rev 12:1).

Yes, truly we can repeat: "O daughter, you are blessed by the Most

High God above all women on earth... walking in the straight path before our God.. .you have avenged our ruin".

Truly indeed, you are blessed.

Yes, here and throughout the Church, in the heart of every individual and in the world as a whole, may you be blessed, O Mary, our sweet Mother.[105]

105 L'Osservatore Romano, Weekly Edition in English May 17, 1982.

Appendix II

Pope John Paul's Third Pilgrimage to Portugal

HOMILY OF HIS HOLINESS POPE JOHN PAUL II

BEATIFICATION OF FRANCISCO AND JACINTA MARTO - SHEPHERDS OF FATIMA
Saturday, 13 May 2000

1. "Father, ... to you I offer praise; for what you have hidden from the learned and the clever you have revealed to the merest children" (Mt 11: 25).

   With these words, dear brothers and sisters, Jesus praises the heavenly Father for his designs; he knows that no one can come to him unless he is drawn by the Father (cf. Jn 6: 44); therefore he praises him for his plan and embraces it as a son: "Yes, Father, for such was your gracious will" (Mt 11: 26). You were pleased to reveal the kingdom to the merest children.

   According to the divine plan, "a woman clothed with the sun" (Rv 12: 1) came down from heaven to this earth to visit the privileged children of the Father. She speaks to them with a mother's voice and heart: she asks them to offer themselves as victims of reparation, saying that she was ready to lead them safely to God. And behold, they see a light shining from her maternal hands which penetrates them inwardly, so that they feel immersed in God just as - they explain - a person sees himself in a mirror. Later Francisco, one of the three privileged children, exclaimed: "We were burning in that light which is God and we were not consumed. What is God like? It is impossible to say. In fact we will never be able to tell people". God: a light that burns without consuming. Moses had the same experience when he saw God in the burning bush; he heard God say that he was concerned about the slavery of his people and had decided to deliver them through him: "I will be with you" (cf. Ex 3: 2-12). Those who welcome this presence become the dwelling-place and, consequently, a "burning bush" of the Most High.

2. What most impressed and entirely absorbed Bl. Francisco was God in that immense light which penetrated the inmost depths of the three children. But God told only Francisco "how sad" he was, as he said. One night his father heard him sobbing and asked him why he was crying; his son answered: "I was thinking of Jesus who is so sad because of the sins that are committed against him". He was motivated by one desire - so expressive of how children think - "to console Jesus and make him happy". A transformation takes place in his life, one we could call radical: a transformation certainly uncommon for children of his age. He devotes himself to an intense spiritual life, expressed in assiduous and fervent prayer, and attains a true form of mystical union with the Lord. This spurs him to a progressive purification of the spirit through the renunciation of his own pleasures and even of innocent childhood games.

Francisco bore without complaining the great sufferings caused by the illness from which he died. It all seemed to him so little to console Jesus: he died with a smile on his lips. Little Francisco had a great desire to atone for the offences of sinners by striving to be good and by offering his sacrifices and prayers. The life of Jacinta, his younger sister by almost two years, was motivated by these same sentiments.

3. "Another portent appeared in heaven; behold, a great red dragon" (Rv 12: 3).

These words from the first reading of the Mass make us think of the great struggle between good and evil, showing how, when man puts God aside, he cannot achieve happiness, but ends up destroying himself.

How many victims there have been throughout the last century of the second millennium! We remember the horrors of the First and Second World Wars and the other wars in so many parts of the world, the concentration and extermination camps, the gulags, ethnic cleansings and persecutions, terrorism, kidnappings, drugs, the attacks on unborn life and the family.

The message of Fátima is a call to conversion, alerting humanity to have nothing to do with the "dragon" whose "tail swept down a third of the stars of heaven, and cast them to the earth" (Rv 12: 4). Man's final goal is heaven, his true home, where the heavenly Father awaits everyone with his merciful love.

God does not want anyone to be lost; that is why 2,000 years ago he sent his Son to earth, "to seek and to save the lost" (Lk 19: 10). And he saved us by his death on the cross. Let no one empty that Cross of its power! Jesus died and rose from the dead to be "the first-born among many brethren" (Rom 8: 29).

In her motherly concern, the Blessed Virgin came here to Fátima to ask men and women "to stop offending God, Our Lord, who is already very offended". It is a mother's sorrow that compels her to speak; the destiny of her children is at stake. For this reason she asks the little shepherds: "Pray, pray much and make sacrifices for sinners; many souls go to hell because they have no one to pray and make sacrifices for them".

4. Little Jacinta felt and personally experienced Our Lady's anguish, offering herself heroically as a victim for sinners. One day, when she and Francisco had already contracted the illness that forced them to bed, the Virgin Mary came to visit them at home, as the little one recounts: "Our Lady came to see us and said that soon she would come and take Francisco to heaven. And she asked me if I still wanted to convert more sinners. I told her yes". And when the time came for Francisco to leave, the little girl tells him: "Give my greetings to Our Lord and to Our Lady and tell them that I am enduring everything they want for the conversion of sinners". Jacinta had been so deeply moved by the vision of hell during the apparition of 13 July that no mortification or penance seemed too great to save sinners.

She could well exclaim with St. Paul: "I rejoice in my sufferings for your sake, and in my flesh I complete what is lacking in Christ's afflictions for the sake of his body, that is, the Church" (Col 1: 24). Last Sunday at the Colosseum in Rome, we commemorated the many witnesses to the faith in the 20th century, recalling the tribulations they suffered through the significant testimonies they left us. An innumerable cloud of courageous witnesses to the faith have left us a precious heritage which must live on in the third millennium. Here in Fátima, where these times of tribulation were foretold and Our Lady asked for prayer and penance to shorten them, I would like today to thank heaven for the powerful witness shown in all those lives. And once again I would like to celebrate the Lord's goodness to me when I was saved from death after being gravely wounded on 13 May 1981.

I also express my gratitude to Blessed Jacinta for the sacrifices and prayers offered for the Holy Father, whom she saw suffering greatly.

5. "Father, to you I offer praise, for you have revealed these things to the merest children". Today Jesus' praise takes the solemn form of the beatification of the little shepherds, Francisco and Jacinta. With this rite the Church wishes to put on the candelabrum these two candles which God lit to illumine humanity in its dark and anxious hours. May they shine on the path of this immense multitude of pilgrims and of all who have accompanied us by radio and television. May Francisco and Jacinta be a friendly light that illumines all Portugal and, in special way, this Diocese of Leiria-Fátima.

I thank Bishop Serafim, of this illustrious particular Church, for his words of welcome, and with great joy I greet the entire Portuguese Episcopate and their Dioceses, which I deeply love and which I urge to imitate their saints. A fraternal greeting goes to the Cardinals and Bishops present, with a special word for the Pastors from the community of Portuguese-speaking countries: may the Virgin Mary obtain reconciliation for the Angolan people; may she bring comfort to the flood victims of Mozambique; may she watch over the steps of Timor Lorosae, Guinea-Bissau, Cape Verde, São Tomé and Príncipe; may she preserve her Brazilian sons and daughters in the unity of faith.

I extend a respectful greeting to the President of the Republic and to the authorities who have wished to take part in this celebration. I take this occasion to express, through them, my gratitude to everyone who helped make my pilgrimage possible. A cordial embrace and a particular blessing to the parish and city of Fátima, which today rejoices in her children who are raised to the honors of the altar.

6. My last words are for the children: dear boys and girls, I see so many of you dressed like Francisco and Jacinta. You look very nice! But in a little while or tomorrow you will take these chothes off and ... the little shepherds will disappear. They should not disappear, should they?! Our Lady needs you all to console Jesus, who is sad because of the bad things done to him; he needs your prayers and your sacrifices for sinners.

Ask your parents and teachers to enroll you in the "school" of Our

Lady, so that she can teach you to be like the little shepherds, who tried to do whatever she asked them. I tell you that "one makes more progress in a short time of submission and dependence on Mary than during entire years of personal initiatives, relying on oneself alone" (St Louis de Montfort, *The True Devotion to the Blessed Virgin Mary*, n. 155). This was how the little shepherds became saints so quickly. A woman who gave hospitality to Jacinta in Lisbon, on hearing the very beautiful and wise advice that the little girl gave, asked who taught it to her. "It was Our Lady", she replied. Devoting themselves with total generosity to the direction of such a good Teacher, Jacinta and Francisco soon reached the heights of perfection.

7. "Father, to you I offer praise, for what you have hidden from the learned and the clever you have revealed to the merest children". Father, to you I offer praise for all your children, from the Virgin Mary, your humble Servant, to the little shepherds, Francisco and Jacinta. May the message of their lives live on for ever to light humanity's way!

Appendix III

ACT OF ENTRUSTMENT OF THE THIRD MILLENIUM TO THE IMMACULATE HEART OF MARY

Jubilee of Bishops
Sunday 8 October 2000

TO THE BISHOPS:

For our support and comfort, we have wished to emphasize during these Jubilee days the presence in our midst of Mary Most Holy, our Mother. We did so yesterday evening by reciting the Rosary as a community; we do so today with the Act of Entrustment, which we will make at the end of Mass. It is an act that we will make in a collegial spirit, while sensing the closeness of the many Bishops who, in their respective sees, are joining in our celebration and making this same Act together with their faithful. May the venerable image of Our Lady of Fátima, which we have the joy of hosting in our midst, help us to relive the experience of the first Apostolic College, gathered in prayer in the Upper Room with Mary, the Mother of Jesus.

Pope John Paul II

1. "Woman, behold your Son!" (Jn 19:26). As we near the end of this Jubilee Year, when you, O Mother, have offered us Jesus anew, the blessed fruit of your womb most pure, the Word made flesh, the world's Redeemer, we hear more clearly the sweet echo of his words entrusting us to you, making you our Mother: "Woman, behold your Son!"

When he entrusted to you the Apostle John, and with him the children of the Church and all people, Christ did not diminish but affirmed anew the role which is his alone as the Savior of the world.

You are the splendor which in no way dims the light of Christ, for you exist in him and through him. Everything in you is fiat: you are the Immaculate One, through you there shines the fullness of grace.

Here, then, are your children, gathered before you at the dawn of the new millennium.

The Church today, through the voice of the Successor of Peter, in union with so many Pastors assembled here from every corner of the world, seeks refuge in your motherly protection and trustingly begs your intercession as she faces the challenges which lie hidden in the future.

2. In this year of grace, countless people have known the overflowing joy of the mercy which the Father has given us in Christ. In the particular Churches throughout the world, and still more in this centre of Christianity, the widest array of people have accepted this gift. Here the enthusiasm of the young rang out, here the sick have lifted up their prayer. Here have gathered priests and religious, artists and journalists, workers and people of learning, children and adults, and all have acknowledged in your beloved Son the Word of God made flesh in your womb. O Mother, intercede for us, that the fruits of this Year will not be lost and that the seeds of grace will grow to the full measure of the holiness to which we are all called.

3. Today we wish to entrust to you the future that awaits us, and we ask you to be with us on our way. We are the men and women of an extraordinary time, exhilarating yet full of contradictions. Humanity now has instruments of unprecedented power: we can turn this world into a garden, or reduce it to a pile of rubble. We have devised the astounding capacity to intervene in the very well-springs of life: man can use this power for good, within the bounds of the moral law, or he can succumb to the short-sighted pride of a science which accepts no limits, but tramples on the respect due to every human being. Today as never before in the past, humanity stands at a crossroads.

And once again, O Virgin Most Holy, salvation lies fully and uniquely in Jesus, your Son.

4. Therefore, O Mother, like the Apostle John, we wish to take you into our home (cf. Jn 19:27), that we may learn from you to become like your Son. "Woman, behold your son!" Here we stand before you to entrust to your maternal care ourselves, the Church, the entire world. Plead for us with your beloved Son that he may give us in abundance the Holy Spirit,

the Spirit of truth which is the fountain of life. Receive the Spirit for us and with us, as happened in the first community gathered round you in Jerusalem on the day of Pentecost (cf. Acts 1:14). May the Spirit open our hearts to justice and love, and guide people and nations to mutual understanding and a firm desire for peace. We entrust to you all people, beginning with the weakest: the babies yet unborn, and those born into poverty and suffering, the young in search of meaning, the unemployed, and those suffering hunger and disease. We entrust to you all troubled families, the elderly with no one to help them, and all who are alone and without hope.

5. O Mother, you know the sufferings and hopes of the Church and the world: come to the aid of your children in the daily trials which life brings to each one, and grant that, thanks to the efforts of all, the darkness will not prevail over the light. To you, Dawn of Salvation, we commit our journey through the new Millennium, so that with you as guide all people may know Christ, the light of the world and its only Saviour, who reigns with the Father and the Holy Spirit for ever and ever. Amen.